TREATING DIFFICULT PERSONALITY DISORDERS

THE JOSSEY-BASS LIBRARY OF CURRENT CLINICAL TECHNIQUE

IRVIN D. YALOM, GENERAL EDITOR

NOW AVAILABLE

Treating Alcoholism
Stephanie Brown, Editor

Treating Schizophrenia
Sophia Vinogradov, Editor

Treating Women Molested in Childhood
Catherine Classen, Editor

Treating Depression
Ira D. Glick, Editor

Treating Eating Disorders
Joellen Werne, Editor

Treating Dissociative Identity Disorder
James L. Spira, Editor

Treating Couples
Hilda Kessler, Editor

Treating Adolescents
Hans Steiner, Editor

Treating the Elderly
Javaid I. Sheikh, Editor

Treating Sexual Disorders
Randolph S. Charlton, Editor

Treating Difficult Personality Disorders
Michael Rosenbluth, Editor

Treating Anxiety Disorders
Walton T. Roth, Editor

Treating the Psychological Consequences of HIV
Michael F. O'Connor, Editor

FORTHCOMING

Treating Children
Hans Steiner, Editor

TREATING DIFFICULT PERSONALITY DISORDERS

A VOLUME IN THE JOSSEY-BASS
LIBRARY OF CURRENT CLINICAL TECHNIQUE

Michael Rosenbluth, EDITOR

Irvin D. Yalom, GENERAL EDITOR

Jossey-Bass Publishers • San Francisco

Substantial discounts on bulk quantities of Jossey-Bass books are available to corporations, professional associations, and other organizations. For details and discount information, contact the special sales department at Jossey-Bass Inc., Publishers (415) 433-1740; Fax (800) 605-2665.

For sales outside the United States, please contact your local Simon & Schuster International Office.

Jossey-Bass Web address: http://www.josseybass.com

Manufactured in the United States of America using Lyons Falls D'Anthology paper, which is a special blend of non-tree fibers and totally chlorine-free wood pulp.

Library of Congress Cataloging-in-Publication Data

Treating difficult personality disorders/Michael Rosenbluth, editor.
     p.   cm.—(Jossey-Bass library of current clinical technique)
     ISBN 0-7879-0315-9 (alk. paper)
     1. Borderline personality disorder—Treatment. 2. Narcissism—Treatment.
     3. Antisocial personality disorders—Treatment. I. Rosenbluth, Michael.
     II. Yalom, Irvin D., date. III. Series.
RC569.5.B67T73 1996
616.8'8506—dc20   96-8761

FIRST EDITION
PB Printing 10 9 8 7 6 5 4 3 2

CONTENTS

FOREWORD

At a recent meeting of clinical practitioners, a senior practitioner declared that more change had occurred in his practice of psychotherapy in the past year than in the twenty preceding years. Nodding assent, the others all agreed.

And was that a good thing for their practice? A resounding "No!" Again, unanimous concurrence—too much interference from managed care; too much bureaucracy; too much paper work; too many limits set on fees, length, and format of therapy; too much competition from new psychotherapy professions.

Were these changes a good or a bad thing for the general public? Less unanimity on this question. Some pointed to recent positive developments. Psychotherapy was becoming more mainstream, more available, and more acceptable to larger segments of the American public. It was being subjected to closer scrutiny and accountability—uncomfortable for the practitioner but, if done properly, of potential benefit to the quality and efficiency of behavioral health care delivery.

But without dissent this discussion group agreed—and every aggregate of therapists would concur—that astounding changes are looming for our profession: changes in the reasons that clients request therapy; changes in the perception and practice of mental health care; changes in therapeutic theory and technique; and changes in the training, certification, and supervision of professional therapists.

From the perspective of the clientele, several important currents are apparent. A major development is the de-stigmatization of psychotherapy. No longer is psychotherapy invariably a hush-hush affair, laced with shame and conducted in offices with separate entrance and exit doors to prevent the uncomfortable possibility of clients meeting one another.

Today such shame and secrecy have been exploded. Television talk shows—Oprah, Geraldo, Donahue—have normalized psychopathology and psychotherapy by presenting a continuous public parade of dysfunctional human situations: hardly a day passes without television fare of confessions and audience interactions with deadbeat fathers, sex addicts, adult children of alcoholics, battering husbands and abused wives, drug dealers and substance abusers, food bingers and purgers, thieving children, abusing parents, victimized children suing parents.

The implications of such de-stigmatization have not been lost on professionals who no longer concentrate their efforts on the increasingly elusive analytically suitable neurotic patient. Clinics everywhere are dealing with a far broader spectrum of problem areas and must be prepared to offer help to substance abusers and their families, to patients with a wide variety of eating disorders, adult survivors of incest, victims and perpetrators of domestic abuse. No longer do trauma victims or substance abusers furtively seek counseling. Public awareness of the noxious long-term effects of trauma has been so sensitized that there is an increasing call for public counseling facilities and a growing demand, as well, for adequate counseling provisions in health care plans.

The mental health profession is changing as well. No longer is there such automatic adoration of lengthy "depth" psychotherapy where "deep" or "profound" is equated with a focus on the earliest years of the patient's life. The contemporary field is more pluralistic: many diverse approaches have proven therapeutically effective and the therapist of today is more apt to tailor the therapy to fit the particular clinical needs of each patient.

In past years there was an unproductive emphasis on territoriality and on the maintaining of hierarchy and status—with the more prestigious professions like psychiatry and doctoral-level psychology expending considerable energy toward excluding master's level therapists. But those battles belong more to the psychotherapists of yesterday; today there is a significant shift toward a more collaborative interdisciplinary climate.

Managed care and cost containment is driving some of these changes. The role of the psychiatrist has been particularly affected as cost efficiency has decreed that psychiatrists will less frequently deliver psychotherapy personally but, instead, limit their activities to supervision and to psychopharmacological treatment.

In its efforts to contain costs, managed care has asked therapists to deliver a briefer, focused therapy. But gradually managed care is realizing that the bulk of mental health treatment cost is consumed by inpatient care and that outpatient treatment, even long-term therapy, is not only salubrious for the patient but far less costly. Another looming change is that the field is turning more frequently toward the group therapies. How much longer can we ignore the many comparative research studies demonstrating that the group therapy format is equally or more effective than higher cost individual therapies?

Some of these cost-driven edicts may prove to be good for the patients; but many of the changes that issue from medical model mimicry—for example, efforts at extreme brevity and overly precise treatment plans and goals that are inappropriate to the therapy endeavor and provide only the illusion of efficiency—can hamper the therapeutic work. Consequently, it is of paramount importance that therapists gain control of their field and that managed care administrators not be permitted to dictate how psychotherapy or, for that matter, any other form of health care be conducted. That is one of the goals of this series of texts: to provide mental health professionals with such a deep grounding in theory and such a clear vision of effective therapeutic technique that they will be empowered to fight confidently for the highest standards of patient care.

The Jossey-Bass Library of Current Clinical Technique is directed and dedicated to the front-line therapist—to master's and doctoral-level clinicians who personally provide the great bulk of mental health care. The purpose of this entire series is to offer state-of-the-art instruction in treatment techniques for the most commonly encountered clinical conditions. Each volume offers a focused theoretical background as a foundation for practice and then dedicates itself to the practical task of what to do for the patient—how to assess, diagnose, and treat.

I have selected volume editors who are either nationally recognized experts or are rising young stars. In either case, they possess a comprehensive view of their specialty field and have selected leading therapists of a variety of persuasions to describe their therapeutic approaches.

Although all the contributors have incorporated the most recent and relevant clinical research in their chapters, the emphasis in these volumes is the practical technique of therapy. We shall offer specific therapeutic guidelines, and augment concrete suggestions with the liberal use of clinical vignettes and detailed case histories. Our intention is not to impress or to awe the reader, and not to add footnotes to arcane academic debates. Instead, each chapter is designed to communicate guidelines of immediate pragmatic value to the practicing clinician. In fact, the general editor, the volume editors, and the chapter contributors have all accepted our assignments for that very reason: a rare opportunity to make a significant, immediate, and concrete contribution to the lives of our patients.

Irvin D. Yalom, M.D.
Professor Emeritus of Psychiatry
Stanford University

INTRODUCTION

Michael Rosenbluth

Difficult personality-disordered patients fill our wards and therapy practices. Most clinicians spend a great deal of their time trying to help these patients, while others try merely to cope with their presence. Still others try to deal with the problem of difficult patients through denial or avoidance: "They should not receive treatment." "They all just have affective disorders." "They're hopeless and untreatable." "I don't treat personality disorders."

Yet these patients do not go away. They are in pain, and they cause pain to their loved ones and their caregivers. They deserve and require our attention. This book offers help to clinicians working with the difficult personality-disordered patient. It focuses on the issues of assessment and treatment that are critical to creating successful therapeutic endeavors and to minimizing the pain that these patients and their therapists can experience in therapy.

The potential for this pain reminds me of Spanish surgeons who refused to give painkillers to gored bullfighters as they cleaned out the bullfighters' wounds. These surgeons believed that the body would heal faster if the bullfighter actually felt the torment of the treatment. I believe that this notion of necessary torment is precisely what we must discard in working with difficult personality-disordered patients. By understanding the specific challenges of caring for these patients, we can feel more competent and comfortable in working with them and can create a safer, less tormented therapeutic environment. If we know how to deal with self-destructive behaviors, countertransference, and treatment selection—to name but a few of the critical issues—we will be more successful in this demanding and difficult therapeutic process.

This volume focuses on the borderline patient as a paradigm of the difficult personality-disordered patient. Chapters Five and Six, on the other hand, look at narcissistic and antisocial patients in order to provide contrast and comparison. By structuring the book in this way, I do not mean to imply that these are the only difficult personality-disordered patients. Instead, the focus allows us to highlight certain principles that will guide our work with all difficult personality-disordered patients.

In addition, the book emphasizes the practical issues that come up in the clinical setting. The authors have avoided academic jargon and speculation and adopted a reader-friendly approach. We focus on the one-to-one therapeutic relationship, including such issues as working with and containing the transference and countertransference that can occur and being flexible enough to augment and mix treatment modalities in order to meet the needs of patients.

OVERVIEW OF THE CONTENTS

The contributors to this volume have been chosen because of their special capacity as educators and clinicians to deepen our understanding of important issues in the care of these difficult patients.

The first chapter, by Dr. Daniel Silver and me, frames some of the relevant clinical issues. We describe several critical challenges in the assessment and treatment of borderline patients, and we encourage therapists to be mindful of the research and clinical experience of others in order to maintain realistic expectations about working with these patients. We introduce the notion of a road map that can help the therapist on the therapeutic journey. Our road map emphasizes careful attention to the assessment process and to such critical challenges as treatment selection, pharmacotherapy, suicidality, and countertransference.

In Chapter Two, Drs. John G. Gunderson, Timothy Davis, and Virginia R. Youngren present a thoughtful discussion of the problems involved in dealing with self-destructive behaviors in borderlines. They emphasize the context in which these behaviors occur and describe useful therapeutic responses to them. Self-destructive behaviors are a particularly chilling challenge to therapists. Perhaps no other issue can compromise therapeutic work as much as does the patient's threat of self-harm. To work with these patients, we must be able to respond effectively to this problem.

In Chapter Three, Dr. Alan Bardikoff looks at the importance of flexibility and responsiveness in working with borderline patients. Difficult personality-disordered patients require therapists to be able to switch gears in order to access all the appropriate modalities that might meet their needs. As therapists we must remember Mark Twain's adage: "If all you have is a hammer, everything looks like a nail." These patients require us to use all the tools in our therapeutic toolbox.

In Chapter Four, Dr. Jerome Kroll makes the point that the basic principles that guide all psychotherapy must also inform the treatment of borderlines. He argues against special treatment, believing that the borderline's reactivity and vulnerability require therapists to pay more, rather than less, attention to the fundamentals of good psychotherapy. He calls for a judicious balance between supportive and exploratory work and between focusing on content and on process. He provides interesting management guidelines for dealing with a patient's previous sexual abuse.

Drs. Gary Rodin and Sam Izenberg, in Chapter Five, focus on patients with Narcissistic Personality Disorder. The authors describe their disenchantment with theory-driven treatments, preferring approaches and models more connected to the subjective experiences of their patients. They conceptualize these patients as suffering primarily from disorders of self-experience; they regard self psychology as a helpful treatment modality. The regulation of self-experience is the focus in this chapter. But this emphasis also applies to clinical treatment of most difficult personality disorders. What is the patient's self-experience? What activities and behaviors are required to maintain it, and what effect does it have on the therapist and the countertransference?

Chapter Six, by Drs. Robert G. Ruegg, Caroline Haynes, and Allen Frances, is a practical and realistic overview of a particularly difficult personality disorder. Certain principles involved in the treatment of Antisocial Personality Disorder are important in the treatment of all difficult personality-disordered patients. The authors address assessment techniques, treatment options, risks of treatment, and legal and ethical issues. They encourage clinicians to be optimistic but realistic in setting goals and, as always, to continue to monitor the countertransference.

Dr. Howard E. Book took up my challenge to write something fresh and reader-friendly on countertransference with the difficult patient. Chapter Seven presents a richly interactive perspective on the critical issue of containing, understanding, and ultimately harnessing the feelings generated in the therapist in order to further the therapeutic work. Dealing with countertransference may be the most critical aspect of working with difficult patients. Because of the sensitivity and volatility of these patients, therapy may be quickly aborted if we are unable to use our countertransference creatively.

Treating difficult personality-disordered patients requires the therapist to be thoughtful, decent, flexible, creative, and pragmatic. These patients, by virtue of their life experiences and psychopathology, often provoke what they most fear: rejection and abandonment. Their inner worlds often cause them to undermine our efforts to help them find what they need in therapy and in life. Nonetheless, these patients remain our best teachers, offering the potential for our most gratifying clinical experiences and deepening our knowledge of the therapeutic process and of ourselves.

ACKNOWLEDGMENTS

It is my great pleasure to acknowledge some of the people who have made a significant contribution to this volume: Dr. Irv Yalom, the editor of this series, who kindly invited me to take on this project; Dr. Molyn Leszcz who encouraged me to put this volume together; Alan Rinzler, my editor at Jossey-Bass, who was a truly remarkable help in the volume's creation; and Barbara Donnelly who provided invaluable clerical and superb organizational support. A special thanks goes to my wife Ronni, who not only helped edit my chapter but enriches everything I do. Last but not least, I would like to thank all the patients with whom I have worked and from whom I have learned so much about therapy, persistence, and courage.

This is dedicated to the ones I love—
Ronni, Sarah, and Daniel
and
Annette and Tadj Rosenbluth

TREATING
DIFFICULT PERSONALITY
DISORDERS

ASSESSMENT AND TREATMENT OF BORDERLINE PERSONALITY DISORDER

Michael Rosenbluth and Daniel Silver

Patients with Borderline Personality Disorder (BPD) present a challenge to their families, themselves, and to the mental health professionals who attempt to help them. About 8 to 10 percent of borderline patients eventually kill themselves, and approximately three quarters make an attempt to do so. Some 15 to 25 percent of psychiatric inpatients and outpatients have BPD. The assessment and treatment of Borderline Personality Disorder is clearly an urgent and critical challenge to mental health professionals.

Freud has described psychotherapy as a journey. We believe the clinical care of the BPD patient can be an especially difficult journey, one that requires a road map that will help clinicians know what to expect of their patients and of themselves along the way.

Specifically, as clinicians we need to know what research has to say about such critical issues as pharmacotherapy and psychotherapy, and we need to look at what guidelines our clinical experiences provide for working with these patients.

The treatment of BPD has seen different fashions come and go over the last few decades. In the literature of the 1970s, Maltsberger and Buie stated that if we can only contain and utilize our countertransference, most BPD patients will do well. In the 1980s, the literature was less optimistic about outcome. In the 1990s, current research urges us to be as careful and thoughtful as possible in integrating pharmacotherapeutic and psychotherapeutic approaches in order to optimize the care of the BPD patient. We feel that careful consideration of the particular challenges of assessment and treatment can provide a road map for our work with these patients.

THE ASSESSMENT PHASE

The assessment phase is critical in the treatment of BPD. Since there is no one treatment that is optimal for every patient, treatment choice must rest on a careful and thorough assessment. There are a number of challenges in the assessment process. These include process issues regarding the duration of and stance taken during the assessment phase, as well as content issues such as diagnostic and treatment choice.

Process Issues in the Assessment Phase

Ideally, the assessment phase should be shorter rather than longer. By its nature, the assessment process shows the clinician in an idealized light. The patient not infrequently experiences the therapist as easygoing, congenial, interactive, and empathic. If at the end of the assessment, the therapist (for any number of reasons) decides to refer the patient on, the "rejection" can have devastating consequences. Furthermore, if the assessment is being done as a consultation for a colleague, it should be kept preferably to one session and never more than two. Because the patient frequently experiences the consultative process as being what he would like his therapy to be, a lengthy assessment by a different therapist has the potential to devalue further the ongoing therapy.

It is important in an assessment not to dig too deeply for material when we are not prepared to follow up ourselves or able to ensure that immediate transfer to a competent therapist will take place. These vulnerable and fragile patients, who may have managed so far to get along in their own particular way, may seriously disintegrate during the course of an insensitive assessment.

In other words, while the assessment process must be used to explore as many areas as possible, we should nevertheless remember that the patient must continue functioning after the assessment has been completed. This is not unlike the responsibility of a surgeon who embarks on a difficult operation, only to realize that it is more complicated and complex than he had anticipated and then walks away, leaving it for his novice assistant to close up. When BPD patients are subjected to a very intensive assessment, we must make sure that there is some closure after the assessment process.

Content Issues in Assessment

Axis I Issues.
Clinical experience and outcome studies indicate that intensive psychotherapy is not for all BPD patients. In addition, Robert Waldinger and John Gunderson's work on completed psychotherapies of these patients suggests that a great number of patients do not remain in intensive psychotherapy beyond six months. Taken together, these considerations suggest the importance of determining any co-morbid Axis I diagnoses so that other potentially useful treatment options can be considered.

One of the main reasons that an Axis I diagnosis is difficult to make in borderline patients is that most clinicians are relatively uninterested in the existence or importance of these diagnoses in this patient population. Often clinicians, particularly of the psychodynamic persuasion, tend to regard BPD as almost precluding an Axis I diagnosis. Once the diagnosis of BPD has been made, they spend less time and energy on assessing whether other diagnoses can also be made. Because anxiety, panic, and depression are common in the BPD presentation and are usually considered simply part of the characterological makeup of these patients, the clinician may neglect to see them as possible symptoms of an Axis I co-morbid diagnosis.

But our assessment must pay close attention to possible Axis I diagnoses. Owing to the BPD patient's dramatic presentation, some clinicians forget that BPD is an Axis II diagnosis and mistakenly consider it an Axis I diagnosis. It is not. We should look beyond the chaotic symptoms of the initial clinical encounter and consider the presence of Axis I diagnoses such as Generalized Anxiety Disorder, Panic Disorder, or Affective Disorder. Although it is more difficult to identify Axis I disorders in the BPD population, it is essential to do so. It is important to take a descriptive history, emphasizing not only the cross-sectional presentation but also exploring the history for discrete, nontransient episodes of depression, anxiety, panic, substance abuse, and other symptomatology. A family history of any psychiatric disorders is relevant, as is previous medication response in the patient and family members. Finally, as Paul Andrulonis's group has shown, it is essential to review the history for signs and symptoms suggesting an organic component. These include trauma, encephalitis, epilepsy, learning and/or attention deficits, and birth trauma.

Affective Disorder. The relationship between BPD and Affective Disorder requires particular attention. While we cannot describe this research in detail here, we will briefly summarize it to provide a context for this important clinical issue.

In two critical papers in 1985 and 1991, Gunderson and Elliot reviewed the considerable amount of research relating to this topic. Essentially, they generated four different hypotheses. One was that BPD causes Affective Disorder. The other was that Affective Disorder causes BPD. The next was that they are not related, and the last was that they are related in a nonspecific way. In 1985, Gunderson and Elliot concluded that they were related in a nonspecific way. They reversed their conclusion in 1991 and stated that they were, in fact, unrelated.

However, even in these important papers summarizing so much information, the considerable correlation between the two disorders was noted, and more to the point, the authors noted that these patients do respond, sometimes dramatically, to antidepressants. This pragmatic clinical observation cannot be overlooked. Particularly with the advent of the new generation of antidepressants—the selective serotonin reuptake inhibitors (SSRIs)—pharmacotherapy is an important aspect of the treatment of BPD.

We also need to remember that the psychodynamic literature has to some degree inadvertently diverted our attention away from the relationship of BPD to Affective Disorder. The literature has distinguished between the different qualities of depression in Major Depressive Disorder and in BPD; this has contributed to the tendency to overlook the presence of depression with BPD.

It is true that in Major Depressive Disorder the patient is more likely to experience a guilty and remorseful depression concerned with issues of defeat and failure, while the BPD depression is psychologically experienced as emptiness, loneliness, and a sensitivity to interpersonal loss. However, this distinction should not diminish the importance of Affective Disorder as an important Axis I diagnosis, as we can see in the following case study:

P . G .

P.G. was a thirty-five-year-old single teacher who had a long history of impulse control problems, marked sensitivity to rejection, mood lability, and difficulty establishing close personal relationships. She had been in several courses of psychotherapy with well-meaning and, by reputation, skilled therapists. Although she felt she had learned something with each course of therapy, her life remained largely unchanged. I (M.R.) met her when she was admitted for a psychiatric day treatment program following a recent hospital admission after she had cut her wrists. The quality of her depression seemed consistent with her borderline personality organization. Yet on taking a careful history, I found that she also met *DSM-IV* criteria for Major Depressive Disorder. I felt that she had never had an adequate trial of antidepressant medication.

She was started on sertraline (an SSRI antidepressant) and required a dose of 150 mg. In the next four weeks, she experienced marked symptom relief of her depression. Over the next few months she described other changes. What was pleasing for her was that she felt that something fundamental had changed in how she experienced herself and others. She felt more "together," less sensitive, and more resilient. She engaged more readily in psychotherapy and felt her efforts were more productive. She was seen two years later, still on antidepressants, still in psychotherapy, and feeling that she was, in ways important for her, more comfortable in her life and her work.

It is important to remember that the personality structure of BPD alters the experience and expression of depression. However, this should not cause us to overlook the presence of Major Depressive Disorder. In other words, as clinicians, we must not focus on the different qualities of the depression so much that we fail to recognize an Axis I diagnosis of Affective Disorder.

We must also remember that many patients who have been seen as having both Affective Disorder and BPD at one point in time have, on four- to seven-year follow-up, no longer met the criteria for BPD. This is encouraging news for front-line clinicians. These patients, who presented with BPD and also had Affective Disorder, on follow-up were only seen to have Affective Disorder. This is a complex and interesting observation, and it is beyond the scope of this chapter to examine it further. However, the "take-home point" is that we do not want to miss the possibility of an Axis I Affective Disorder, especially since some of our patients may, with time, "outgrow" their personality disorder (or may not truly have had it to begin with). The following case provides an example.

F . G .

F.G. was a twenty-four-year-old female who experienced marked tantrums, identity difficulties, rapidly fluctuating and unsuccessful relationships with men, recurrent suicidal behaviors (wrist cutting and overdoses), and mood instability and reactivity. She had multiple hospitalizations following her relationship failures and accompanying self-harm behaviors. A careful evaluation suggested that the BPD diagnosis and management problems had diverted attention from a Bipolar Affective Disorder.

She was seen eight years later, and both she and her therapist reported that aggressive treatment of her bipolar disorder (lithium carbonate and antidepressants as required) had permitted her to reduce her need for hospitalization dramatically (she had been hospitalized twice in the past eight years versus an average of two or three hospitalizations a year prior to that). She still required psychotherapy to deal with her characterological vulnerabilities (a fear of intimacy and rejection sensitivity), but she no longer met the diagnostic criteria for BPD.

Thus, BPD patients remind us to remain good overall clinicians, able to assess Axis I disorders even in the context of a difficult personality organization. Although the personality organization will affect the treatment of Major Depressive Disorder, having a clear Axis I diagnosis does invite the clinician to use the indicated combination of psychotherapy and pharmacotherapy to treat the Axis I disorder. It is still easier to treat Axis I disorders than Axis II disorders. Certainly, overlooking the Axis I disorder will *not* facilitate the treatment of BPD.

Social Supports.   Assessing the patient's social supports is an important undertaking. The assessment phase requires careful evaluation of the patient's external world. Do important friends or relatives still care about the patient, or are they fed up with her, almost wishing she were dead? (The mother of one BPD adolescent who killed himself struggled for years afterward with guilt about her conscious wishes that he would die.) Has there been any significant change in work or school that affects the patient's social context and that may color the presenting symptoms? Are there other therapeutically linked events, such as discharge from hospital, group therapy, or agency involvement, that may impinge on the patient's relative cohesion and stability?

These factors require careful assessment for at least two reasons. First, identifying such events can facilitate a brief psychotherapy by focusing on the meaning of the loss for the patient and on what it evokes for him. Remember, for patients who often have chaotic lives, therapy can become mired in a multitude of difficulties. By looking closely at the state of social supports and their meaning for the patient, we establish a useful and circumscribed focus. For some patients, this helps avoid the malignant regressions and acting out that can occur in an open-ended therapy.

Second, the presence or absence of sustaining individuals and social structures is an important factor in choosing therapeutic strategies. Some patients require a therapeutic emphasis on their external context, and therapeutic efforts are directed at building social or vocational supports, rather than exploring the patient's inner world. However, even those patients who are candidates for intensive psychological exploration require careful monitoring of their social supports. These supports can have a crucial impact on both the patient's and the therapist's capacity to weather the difficulties that so often characterize the therapeutic journey with BPD. The patient who has a stable, albeit tumultuous, relationship with a partner is not alone in her life and so is not alone with the therapist.

J . D .

J.D. was a thirty-one-year-old woman when she began twice-a-week therapy. She had marked difficulties in her life both professionally and personally. The therapy was quite tumultuous due to intense abandonment sensitivity, affective instability, chronic feelings of emptiness (she felt to an *almost* delusional degree that she had a hole in her heart), and intense anger when she felt unappreciated or unlistened to. I (M.R.) found her difficult because of her neediness, anger, and storminess. Yet after eight years of two- and sometimes three-times-a-week therapy, she moved forward dramatically in her life.

She completed her professional training, married the strong, silent (she felt schizoid) boyfriend who had stood by her in all her difficulties, and felt pleased with her accomplishments in therapy and in her life. My own review of her treatment identified many factors that were important in the positive outcome, including her intelligence, our relative compatibility and persistence, and her boyfriend. I believe that his ongoing presence in her life throughout the therapy permitted both J.D. and me to feel that we were not totally alone with each other in the therapy. This realization was crucial, in different ways, for each of us.

TREATMENT CHOICE

Choosing the optimum treatment for your BPD patient is critical. Several important aspects must be considered.

Long Term or Brief?

Long-term exploratory psychotherapy was once considered the optimal treatment modality for BPD. To some extent this reflected work with healthier BPD patients who were seen in office psychotherapy practice and who rarely, if ever, needed hospitalization. Experience with more severe BPD patients suggests that long-term therapy may be indicated for a small minority of them. Certainly new economic realities (managed care and so on) make long-term exploratory therapy the exception, not the rule.

In addition, not all patients remain in, or benefit from, exploratory psychotherapy. Waldinger and Gunderson surveyed psychiatrists and psychoanalysts with an average of twenty years' experience and with a particular interest and commitment to BPD patients (as demonstrated by their contributions to the literature in this area). In this elite group of therapists (eleven of twelve of whom were psychoanalysts), they found that only 50 percent of patients stayed in treatment beyond six months, and of those who remained in treatment, only a minority were deemed by the therapist to have benefited.

This study can be interpreted in a number of ways. One reading suggests that we must be careful when we recommend long-term psychotherapy and remember the importance of considering other therapeutic modalities and adjuncts to psychotherapy.

We also think it is reasonable to consider that this study suggests that briefer therapies may be more suitable for BPD patients. Particularly interesting is the finding that those who did benefit from long-term psychotherapy often had three or four previous psychotherapeutic experiences that perhaps prepared them for the more definitive involvement.

Key Indicators

The literature has suggested a variety of indicators that can help predict for which patients psychotherapy is most appropriate. Empirical validation of these different indicators has been slow in coming. Whatever indices are used, the purpose of the assessment process is to determine the degree to which therapy can achieve such treatment goals as developing a more cohesive sense of self; strengthening the BPD patient's sense of identity;

increasing the capacity for relationships; decreasing feelings of emptiness, despair, alienation, and disintegration; decreasing the degree of chronic feelings of rage; and decreasing needy, clingy, demanding, or paranoid stances, while increasing the capacity for trust.

Traditional indicators, such as impulsiveness or suicide attempts, have not proved accurate as predictors of outcome with this group of patients. Our own clinical impressions and research endeavors seem to indicate that the assessment of certain relationship capacities may be more useful for treatment decisions.

One of us (D.S.) has described previous relationship capacity as a prime determinant in whether exploratory psychotherapy should be undertaken. A history of no meaningful relationships, little capacity for being soothed, or difficulty being empathic to others suggests the patient is not a candidate for depth approaches.

Clinically we have found that the capacity to be soothed appears to have an important association for psychotherapy outcome, while its absence seems to be correlated with very poor outcome. If we review our therapies, the patients who could attach and be comforted (by teddy bears or favorite pets, for example) are overrepresented among good-outcome BPD patients.

In everyday parlance, "to soothe" is to bring comfort, solace, or peace. In clinical practice, we often find that a patient who is greatly distressed or in turmoil can derive soothing and comfort from the natural course of psychotherapy itself, without recourse to special interventions. It is this capacity to feel psychologically soothed or comforted that is most important in predicting psychotherapy outcome. Therefore, the assessing therapist needs to review which relationships, personal or therapeutic, have been able to provide any comfort or solace to the patient.

For the patient who has had no experience of being comforted in any relationship, intensive uncovering therapy is usually contraindicated. To elicit a stark awareness of this irreparable defect without providing other alternatives or supports can make the patient feel dangerously despairing, empty, and futile, and may even increase the risk of suicide. The way to determine the presence or lack of the capacity to be soothed is to take a careful history, identifying whether there has been some relationship, perhaps even in the distant past, such as a concerned or interested teacher, a loving grandparent, or some other adult who provided at least one important experience of soothing, comforting, solacing, that may have been forgotten after many years of difficulties. If this relationship existed, the capacity to be soothed may become available during the psychotherapeutic process.

The potential for developing a good therapeutic relationship can also be determined in the course of an assessment interview. It is important to take a relationship history to determine the quality of the relationships that the person has been able to sustain. The absence of the capacity to sustain at least one meaningful and nondestructive relationship in either a personal, work, or social situation for a minimum of one year between adolescence and the current assessment period suggests that an uncovering type of therapy should rarely be undertaken.

It is also important to assess the capacity for empathy, which requires the therapist to explore fully the patient's thoughts, feelings, and perceptions of significant others. The term *empathy* has suffered from overuse in the psychiatric literature. Empathy is defined here as the patient's interpersonal capacity to tune in to others, or to be tuned in to by others, cognitively and affectively. Part of the assessment involves determining whether an empathic therapeutic bridge can be established between therapist and patient.

Thus, we must determine with the patient whether he can empathize with important people in his life. Some patients can only give a negative description of a hostile, intrusive, and punitive parent, without being able to offer any kind of understanding as to why their parent was that way. This can be a useful index of the patient's capacity to empathize and understand other people's experience, even those who have had a harmful effect on him. The absence of capacity to empathize suggests that such a patient is not going to do as well in long-term intensive psychotherapy.

Previous Therapeutic Experiences

As just described, the capacity to establish a relationship is an important prognostic indicator with regard to starting psychotherapy. One category of relationships to consider, especially in the BPD patient, is previous therapeutic experience. Basic transference constellations involving frustration, disappointments, and the patient's defenses against these affects can be elicited in the assessment process by reviewing previous therapeutic relationships.

V.J.

V.J. was a thirty-eight-year-old woman with a long history of difficulties with men, social hunger yet social isolation, self-harm behaviors, and anger-management difficulties. She sought treatment with me because she hoped I would be different from her two previous therapists. She'd found the first one to be "too hard" and ungiving. She ended treatment after three years. She found the second therapist "too soft"—she felt he was too kind and indulgent. She hoped I would be "just right."

It was helpful that she could reflect on her perceptions of her two previous therapists, and she related these to her experiences of her father while she was growing up (which had been full of betrayal and pain). My own view was that I was probably too much like the second therapist, and I felt it would be best for her to undergo more intensive psychotherapy than I could provide at the time.

Follow-up with her therapist a few years later indicated that she had met with some success. She was able to modulate some of her difficulties, and her relationship capacity with men had improved. She was more aware of how her perceptions of her previous therapists had been colored, to some extent, by her transference vulnerabilities.

SPECIAL TREATMENT CHALLENGES

Therapists must be clear about special treatment challenges on the therapeutic journey with BPD patients. We will add to our road map here by looking at the issues of pharmacotherapy, self-destructive behavior, and countertransference.

Pharmacotherapy

We have already emphasized the importance of recognizing Axis I disorders in the assessment of BPD patients. An Axis I diagnosis offers the clinician a chance to deal with something somewhat simpler than the personality organization of the patient. The usual combination of pharmacotherapy and psychotherapy is called for with the particular Axis I disorders.

Clinicians should remember that BPD patients may benefit from medication. The research on pharmacotherapy in BPD is long and complicated. It may be helpful to summarize the gist of it. First, there is a school of research that is interested in whether psychoactive medications can affect the personality disorder itself, even when there is no Axis I disorder present. The early returns from this research are mixed. We believe clinicians are on safer ground if a formal Axis I disorder can be identified, using *DSM-IV* criteria, and then treated with the appropriate medications. This is the categorical approach to diagnosis. When you are unable to identify a formal Axis I disorder, then it is reasonable to consider whether or not domains of disorders or subclinical thresholds are met that can guide medication trials. This is the dimensional approach to diagnosis. The term *dimensional* refers to the search for clinical clusters or dimensions of a problem that can organize our thinking.

Thus, if one is unable to make an Axis I diagnosis in the BPD patient, one would then look for a cognitive perceptual domain, an affective domain, an impulsive behavioral domain, or an anxiety domain. It is worthwhile for nonmedical clinicians to be aware of these clinical dimensions and the medication options available for them.

The cognitive perceptual domain refers to a BPD presentation where there are some ideas of reference or delusional thinking. In this case an antipsychotic might be of some help. Low-dose antipsychotic medications (neuroleptics) have been found to be clinically useful in organizing the patient and, in particular, organizing the ideas of reference and delusions. These medications are effective but have the risk of tardive dyskinesia, a gradually developing movement disorder that is irreversible and occurs in a small percentage of patients on long-term antipsychotic medication. Thus, the clinician would want to keep in mind the possibility of prescribing a low-dose neuroleptic, but should not rush to use it nor use it for a prolonged period of time. Nonetheless, the clinician would not want to avoid using it in a situation where a patient does indeed have some psychotic symptomatology or vulnerability and would benefit from some reduction in these symptoms.

The affective domain has already been covered. Essentially this occurs in some patients who do not formally meet Axis I criteria for Major Depressive Disorder. These patients might, however, meet criteria for Dysthymia; BPD patients frequently do. Dysthymia is a chronic low-grade depression in which, by *DSM-IV* definition, less than five of nine depressive symptoms are present more days than not in a two-year period.

Consideration could be given to selective serotonin reuptake inhibitors (SSRIs). Tricyclics have not been especially helpful and are dangerous in overdose. The new antidepressants—the SSRIs such as Zoloft—are more helpful for these patients in general and in affective domain in particular; they also have the marked advantage of being safe in overdose, certainly much safer than the other antidepressants. Monoamine oxidase (MAO) inhibitors have traditionally been helpful in this domain but are problematic because patients taking them have to monitor their diet carefully to avoid hypertensive reactions. They also are not safe in overdose.

The pragmatic point is that when you suspect that there is an affective domain—but not a formal Axis I disorder—present in a BPD patient, you should refer him to a psychiatrist for medication assessment.

The impulsive behavioral domain refers to the BPD patient who is markedly impulsive, binge eats, is aggressive, or has tantrums. This is a familiar domain for clinicians working with BPD. These patients may sometimes also have EEG abnormalities. There is a suggestion in the literature that these abnormalities may be related to a subgroup of BPD patients who are what we may term "wired differently." They may have learning disabilities, birth trauma, or encephalitis. An anticonvulsant medication such as carbamazepine is worth a try on this type of patient. Once again, none of these medications is a magic bullet for these disorders but should be used as part of an integrated treatment approach, where psychotherapy can be facilitated and enhanced by the stabilizing and therapeutic effects of medication.

Last, there is the anxious domain, where patients have signs and symptoms of anxiety as their main clinical expression and yet do not meet the criteria for Generalized Anxiety Disorder or Panic Disorder. For this population, a long-acting anti-anxiety medication, such as clonazepam, is worth keeping in mind. This can settle the patient's anxiety symptoms, allowing her to feel more internally cohesive and less vulnerable to the marked anxieties that tend to disorganize her.

The use of medications can become grist for the therapeutic mill. If a medical colleague is prescribing, the stage may be set for splitting to occur (for example, the prescribing doctor might be seen as "good," and the therapist might be seen as "bad"). These splits can be anticipated, rather than played into, and when they occur, they can be managed helpfully. Careful dialogue with the prescribing doctor helps avert them. Another medication-related issue is that the patient's cycle of idealization and devaluation can be played out with the medications themselves. Thus, it is important to set the stage for the use of medication, to set realistic expectations about what these medications can and cannot do, and to help the patient participate in reasonable medication trials. (Often the first medication will not be helpful, but the second or third one might be.) For some patients, having a concrete focus like medication can be quite helpful. Certainly, any therapeutic improvement that a robust, or even partial, drug response may offer is appreciated by patient and therapist alike.

Last, we should emphasize that the SSRIs are an important advance in the medication approach of these patients. Unlike their tricyclic precursors, SSRIs are safe in overdose. This is particularly important in this patient population.

Self-Destructive Behavior

Self-destructive behavior is one of the most vexing and difficult challenges in working with the BPD patient. Different people have advocated different measures, from nonintervention to consistent intervention when this occurs. Otto Kernberg has even gone so far as to have patients sign a contract that removes therapists from liability for the patients' self-harm behaviors or deaths by suicide. Most of us, however, do not have the luxury of such contracts with our patients.

We have to understand, and help the patient understand in no uncertain terms, that we as therapists cannot take responsibility for the patient's life. As these patients are frequently not only acutely suicidal but chronically suicidal, we must be clear that ultimately the therapeutic task is to help our patients be able to take responsibility for their own lives, rather than look to others to do so. Here is an example:

A . C .

A.C. was a thirty-three-year-old married woman who was in therapy with Dr. B., a young psychiatrist whom I was supervising. Dr. B. found that her patient's repeated suicide threats and occasional behaviors were extremely hard on both of them. She endeavored to be empathic but found that she did not look forward to her sessions with A.C., and she feared phone calls in which A.C. described her pain, desperation, and/or suicide attempts.

Dr. B. was encouraged to set limits with A.C. She stressed that the self-harm behaviors must diminish within the next three months; if they did not, this would suggest that therapy was not helping A.C. Dr. B. indicated that A.C. could reach out but must try her best not to act out. If this was not possible, Dr. B. would help arrange a referral to another therapist.

The self-harm behaviors soon diminished and then ceased. Treatment continued and was not easy. However, both the patient and the therapist felt safer.

It must be made clear at the outset of the therapy that self-harm behaviors that occur in the course of the therapy will signal to both the therapist and the patient that the therapy is not working and that it will have to be reassessed and possibly discontinued. Patients usually find this a helpful and clear message.

Our willingness to intervene in self-destructive episodes must be accompanied by clear and repeated instructions that life-threatening behavior harms the process of therapy. The therapist must convey firmly that he is unable and unwilling to take responsibility for the patient's life. Furthermore, we must convey to the patient that harming herself to elicit help from others is not the way to find out if therapists or others care about her.

Documentation of Suicidality. Other issues related to suicidality are explored in detail in Chapter Two. But before leaving this discussion of self-destructive behavior, we need to look at another aspect of safety.

The literature traditionally discusses suicidality in terms of how we as therapists can help the patient remain safe. But an important aspect of helping the patient feel safe is to help ourselves feel safe. We live in a litigious time; it is of utmost importance that we know how to protect ourselves from a medical-legal perspective so that we do not fear working with these patients more than we need to. Patients can sense when a safe environment has been created in which therapy can occur, and they are helped by this sense of safety (as are therapists!).

We have had the disheartening experience of reviewing records of therapists who were being sued for malpractice. The records often show that the therapist has struggled to help a difficult patient, but they are often extremely poor when it comes to documenting self-harm risk and behaviors and the response of the therapist.

We believe this reflects our lax standards with regard to documentation. This is particularly unfortunate with BPD patients, where self-harm behaviors are a frequent occurrence. We must understand the importance of good documentation. It is an essential part of our skills and professional standards as therapists.

With BPD patients we advocate—in addition to the usual documentation of the content and process of sessions—commenting on the presence or absence of self-harm intent or ideation, particularly if the patient is not in a positive frame of mind. This should become as reflexive as a written "tic," something you do in every note regarding the care of your BPD patient. Related to this, we need a formal protocol for commenting on the continuum of suicidal risk. Most clinicians are familiar with the spectrum from no suicidality, to *tedium vitae* (tired of living), through thoughts reflecting hopelessness and despair, to passive ideation, to nonspecific or specific plans, to attempts past and recent, to actually going to a bridge, and so on.

What clinicians find more challenging is documenting when the patient is chronically suicidal. Our own standard is to indicate that there is no self-harm ideation or intent currently present and the individual has future plans (for work, play, and so on). However, we may note that the patient, although not acutely suicidal at this time, remains a chronic risk, particularly should he use drugs or alcohol or experience further disappointment. We think this realistically covers the possibility of chronic suicidality. We will then note whether hospitalization was required, offered, or accepted by the patient and, if he refused the offer, whether he was certifiable or not.

Last, we encourage health care providers to be mindful of internal consistency with charting. If you see a patient within a day treatment unit, it is important that the psychologist, social worker, nursing staff, and psychiatrist all provide consistent notes regarding suicidality. If one individual documents that the patient is suicidal, this should prompt a verbal message to another member of the team so that the appropriate steps can be taken.

One of us (M.R.) recently reviewed the file of a patient who committed suicide one week after his doctor discharged him from the hospital. The deceased's family lodged a professional complaint against the doctor. Unfortunately for this physician, the nursing notes indicated that the patient was quite suicidal, yet this had not been conveyed to the physician, nor had he noticed it in his work with the patient.

Countertransference

The issue of countertransference is an especially critical one for clinicians working with BPD patients. This issue is covered in detail in Chapter Seven, but it is a topic of such crucial importance that it cannot be overemphasized. Certainly, if we wish to provide a road map for our clinical journey, we must point out its importance.

It is a critical challenge for the therapist working with BPD patients to recognize the feelings induced by the patient and to harness these feelings for the therapeutic task. In particular, self-destructive behavior, defensive strategies used by BPD patients (projection, projective identification, and splitting), and the strong tendency to spoil positive experiences all generate very intense and difficult feelings in the therapist.

It is helpful to have a conceptual framework that permits you to decode these feelings and recognize them as expressions of the patient's inner world. We may say that the BPD patient consciously, or unconsciously, causes the therapist to experience the patient's inner feelings because she is unable to talk about them. By decoding these feelings, the therapist can then help the patient find words to express the feelings she could not previously articulate.

When the therapist recognizes the feelings that have been evoked by the patient, he has the ability not to act on them. Unrecognized countertransference can cause the therapist to distance himself (even to the point of premature termination) or to become too submissive to the patient due to reaction formation and thus accept inexcusable abuse from the patient.

Working with BPD patients can be extremely taxing, and it is important to recognize the maximum number of such patients one can work with effectively at any one time. This number is influenced by the therapist's temperament and capacity, as well as by personal and professional factors in the therapist's life that enhance or diminish the capacity to be effective. Therapists are not immune to the normal difficulties in life, such as marital problems, serious illness, behavioral difficulties in children, and financial problems. Thus, there are some years when we are simply better able to handle more difficult BPD patients. We must recognize our capacity and make some effort to be guided by it. Last, please remember that when you carry too many BPD patients, your other patients will suffer. It is also possible that your family may suffer. You may end up using them inordinately for your own containment.

❧

BPD patients are a difficult group to treat. They require our help and attention, but the nature of their life experience and/or psychopathology often causes them to undermine our efforts to give them what they need. They often provoke what they most fear—rejection and abandonment. In this chapter we have suggested that we can have more successful therapeutic experiences with this needy and deserving patient population if we keep in mind a road map that can guide us on the clinical journey. Such a road map, while it cannot document all the pitfalls and detours or predict unexpected storms, nevertheless must always emphasize careful attention to the assessment process and an awareness of the challenges that the BPD patient poses. Such a recognition helps the clinician stay involved and helpful. Although we have, of necessity, focused on the difficulties of the journey, these patients offer the potential for our richest and most gratifying clinical experiences!

NOTES

P. 1, *About 8 to 10 percent:* Stone, M. H., Hurt, S. W., & Stone, D. K. (1987). The PI 500: Long-term follow-up of borderline inpatients meeting *DSM-III* criteria. *Journal of Personality Disorders, 1,* 291–298.

P. 1, *Some 15 to 25 percent:* Gunderson, J. G. (1984). *Borderline personality disorder.* Washington, DC: American Psychiatric Press.

P. 1, *In the literature of the 1970s:* Maltsberger, J. T., & Buie, D. H. (1974). Countertransference hate in the treatment of suicidal patients. *Archives of General Psychiatry, 30,* 625–633.

P. 3, *Robert Waldinger and John Gunderson's work:* Waldinger, R. J., & Gunderson, J. G. (1984). Completed psychotherapies with borderline patients. *American Journal of Psychotherapy, 38,* 190–202.

P. 4, *Finally, as Paul Andrulonis's:* Andrulonis, P. A., Glueck, B. C., Stroebel, C. F., Vogel, N. G., Shapiro, A. L., & Aldridge, D. M. (1981). Organic brain dysfunction and the borderline syndrome. *The Psychiatric Clinics of North America, 4*(1), 47–66.

P. 4, *In two critical papers:* Gunderson, J. G., & Elliot, G. R. (1985). The interface between Borderline Personality Disorder and Affective Disorder.

American Journal of Psychiatry, 142, 277–288; Gunderson, J. G., & Phillips, K. A. (1991). A current view of the interface between Borderline Personality Disorder and depression. *American Journal of Psychiatry, 148,* 967–975.

P. 10, *Waldinger and Gunderson:* Waldinger, R. J., & Gunderson, J. G. (1984). *ibid.*

P. 11, *One of us:* Silver, D., Glassman, E. F., & Cardish, R. J. (1988). The assessment of the capacity to be soothed: Clinical and methodological issues. In P. Horton, H. Gerwirtz, & K. Kreutter (Eds.), *The solace paradigm: An eclectic search for psychological immunity* (pp. 2–10). Madison, CT: International Universities Press.

P. 16, *The impulsive behavioral domain:* Andrulonis, P. A., Glueck, B. C., Stroebel, C. F., Vogel, N. G., Shapiro, A. L., & Aldridge, D. M. (1981). *ibid.*

P. 17, *Otto Kernberg has even gone so far:* Kernberg, O., Selzer, M. A., Koenigsberg, H. W., Carr, A. C., & Applebaum, A. H. (1989). *Psychodynamic psychotherapy of borderline patients.* New York: Basic Books.

2

DEALING WITH SELF-DESTRUCTIVENESS IN BORDERLINE PATIENTS

John G. Gunderson, Timothy Davis, and Virginia R. Youngren

For better or worse, the term *borderline* evokes an immediate reaction from most mental health professionals. While it is in the nature of borderline patients to elicit strong responses from those around them, we believe that much of the reflexive dread experienced by some clinicians stems more from a lack of understanding of these complex patients than from anything inherently dreadful about the patients themselves. In working with these patients at McLean Hospital, we have concluded that although a little knowledge can be a dangerous thing, even less knowledge can be deadly.

Self-destructive behavior is one of the defining characteristics of these patients. Repeated suicide attempts and self-mutilation comes closest to representing the "behavioral specialty" that can fix the borderline diagnosis in the clinician's mind. Indeed, it has become the norm for clinicians to use the borderline diagnosis whenever a patient with repeated suicide attempts is assessed.

Chapter adapted from Gunderson, J. (1984). Self-destructiveness in borderline patients, *Borderline Personality Disorder* (pp. 85–99). Washington, DC: American Psychiatric Press. Reprinted by permission.

Not surprisingly, self-destructiveness is also the characteristic of the borderline patient's psychopathology that generates the most stress in those who attempt to help him. Perhaps nothing inspires young therapists more than the chance to fulfill the literal promise of their profession and, more generally, one of life's most valued enterprises—saving an endangered life. For therapists who adopt such a clinical mission, there are very few experiences that will be as painful as the seemingly spiteful efforts of borderline patients alternately to extend and then to deny the hope that this ambition will be fulfilled.

This chapter addresses the nature and extent of this self-destructive activity by borderline patients, the context in which these behaviors occur, and what constitutes a useful therapeutic approach to this problem. It is our hope that with more understanding, clinicians will also develop greater comfort and clarity of thought in working with these patients as well as in dealing with their own reactions to them.

SELF-DESTRUCTIVE BEHAVIORS

When we talk about self-destructiveness, we are talking about behaviors that are both diverse and exceedingly common in this patient population. In an early study conducted at McLean Hospital, we found that almost 75 percent of a sample of fifty-seven patients with Borderline Personality Disorder had made suicide threats prior to admission; 70 percent had taken an overdose, most frequently of a barbiturate; almost 65 percent had mutilated themselves by cutting, banging, burning, or puncturing their body; 67 percent had abused drugs or alcohol; another 67 percent had been involved in sexual promiscuity; and 25 percent had been involved in accident-prone, reckless behavior.

It is our experience that wrist slashing, the most common form of self-mutilation, is more common in females than males, whereas no such gender-related pattern is evident in the case of overdoses.

It is more difficult to generalize about the self-destructive intent of promiscuity, drug abuse, and accidents. Often the interviewer considered these acts more self-destructive than did the patients. Therapists also recognize the more subtle and recurrent evidences of a ubiquitous—albeit less dangerous—self-destructiveness in the everyday life of borderline patients. Characteristic of many of these instances is that the patients themselves ignore the potential dangers or deny any self-destructive intention despite how obvious it is to those around them.

We worked with one such patient who seemed quite oblivious to the adverse consequences of her behavior.

MELANIE

Melanie, twenty-four and intermittently a student at a community college, was well known to the inpatient psychiatric staff of the local general hospital where she had been admitted on three recent occasions. In each case, admission followed an altercation with her parents about rules at home and the man whom she was dating.

Melanie's boyfriend was a musician in his late thirties, who was occasionally employed. Melanie's parents disapproved of this man and his apparent lack of direction. They took the position that while Melanie lived under their roof, she needed to abide by their rules. In particular, they imposed a curfew and forbade the use of drugs in the house. Melanie strongly resisted the idea of a curfew and, when confronted by her parents, would storm out of the house and stay out for days at a time.

When she did eventually call home, she would report that she and her boyfriend had been using crack, and she was feeling hopeless and suicidal. Her mother would insist that she be hospitalized. Once Melanie was in the hospital, the staff observed that she would tend to compose herself and recover her energy relatively quickly. She would begin to argue with the nurses and with her parents about visits from her boyfriend and within short order be discharged, often in the midst of controversy about what she was going to be doing when she returned home.

As this vignette suggests, there is often a "power struggle" underlying threats of suicide in these patients, with the threat or gesture of suicide exerting a coercive force on the person to whom it is directed. In our study, forty-three of the fifty-seven patients were considered to have made at least one manipulative suicide attempt. These attempts were considered manipulative on the basis of their having been carried out, usually repetitiously, under circumstances where their rescue would be likely and that seemed designed to exact some saving response from a specific other person. The three most common explanations given by borderline patients for these attempts were rage at another person, a wish to punish oneself, and a state of panic.

Gestures and Threats Versus Completions

While most suicidal gestures and threats are just that—gestures and threats—we urge you to keep in mind the very real risk of completed suicide in this group of patients. Studies have estimated the lifetime prevalence of completed suicide in this population to be about 9 percent. This is comparable to the rates for Affective Disorders and Schizophrenia and is higher in those borderline patients who suffer from co-morbid Affective Disorder or substance abuse. According to these studies, the risk diminishes with time.

Recently, we took part in a study at McLean Hospital that showed that suicidal behavior declined precipitously over the five-year follow-up period while self-destructive behavior declined only modestly, and both suicidal and self-destructive ideation remained essentially unchanged. These findings suggest that there is little, if any, correlation between suicidal ideation and suicidal behavior. Similarly, self-destructive behavior does not predict suicidal behavior in any consistent manner. These two unfortunate facts contribute to the complexity and challenge of understanding and treating the borderline patient.

The Critical Role of Relationships

The appearance of self-destructive behavior can often be understood in terms of the patient's relationship to an important "primary" person in his or her life. When such relationships are going smoothly and one or more significant people are present and supportive, the patient may exhibit depressive features but will refrain from serious self-destructive behaviors. When a relationship is frustrating, the patient may react with manipulative threats and suicidal gestures. In the absence of a sustaining relationship, impulsive or psychotically driven self-destructive behaviors are common.

When Relationships Are Frustrating

When one of these significant (we might well say crucial) others is frustrating to the borderline person or when the specter of their loss is raised, then the angry, devaluative, and manipulative features predominate. These are the circumstances under which manipulative suicidal gestures and threats become frequent. These suicidal gestures are accompanied by angry or despairing affect. They represent efforts to keep the person from leaving and prevent the dreaded consequences of her loss.

Self-destructive acts here are directed more interpersonally. Often the acts express anger and are designed to hurt a frustrating person (sadism). Following a phone conversation in which his mother refused to visit him that evening, Michael drank a quart of whiskey and took six sleeping pills. At two o'clock in the morning, he phoned his mother and with slurred speech told her what he had done. Twenty minutes later, in a state of panic, she arrived at his apartment and found him with blood oozing from his arms where he had just cut himself.

Another type of self-destructive behavior that we have commonly encountered expresses desperation designed to gain the attention and protective intervention of others (a cry for help). When Jo learned that her boyfriend wanted to break up with her and date other women, she took a handful of aspirin and called some mutual friends. The friends first ensured that she got medical attention, then provided her with emotional support and helped her to tolerate the change in her boyfriend's feelings.

A third category of self-destructive acts expresses both anger and desperation in order to coerce another into compliance with the patient's needs (manipulation). During a therapy session, Meagan repeatedly spoke of her plans to commit suicide and challenged her therapist to hospitalize her involuntarily. When her therapist instead insisted that she take responsibility for the decision to go into the hospital, Meagan took a small mirror out of her pocketbook, broke it on the arm of her chair, and superficially cut herself with the broken glass.

In some instances, patients whose original self-destructive behavior was accompanied by rage or despair later learn to employ the same act in a more purely manipulative manner as a result of the unexpectedly gratifying response they received earlier. For example, Melanie, the patient mentioned earlier, initially despaired of living at home under her parents' rules but found their forceful response to her running away and using drugs to be gratifying. Over time she learned that she could manipulate her mother into showing concern by running away and then making a panicked call home. As noted, these interpersonal functions are especially characteristic of self-destructive behavior that occurs when a significant relationship is frustrating or a separation is imminent; they can be understood as an effort to reassert a sense of power and control over that important person.

When Relationships Are Missing

When a borderline patient feels an absence or lack of any primary relationship, then psychotic phenomena or intolerable states of aloneness may occur. The patient no longer feels depression or rage; he is terrified and panicked. To avoid these intense feelings, he may engage in several forms of self-destructive activity. These may appear the same as those just described, which are interpersonal and manipulative in nature, but they now occur with different functions and require different therapeutic interventions.

To stave off the panic associated with the absence of an important other, borderline patients will engage impulsively in behaviors that numb the panic and establish contact with and control over some new person. Fights and promiscuity, often assisted by the disinhibiting influence of drugs or alcohol, are common and potentially quite dangerous even though their intent is not self-injurious.

If such activities are unavailable or if they fail to establish the needed contact, then dissociative phenomena may occur, and another type of self-destructive action may ensue. Dissociative experiences accompanied by nihilistic fear (for example, "Am I dead?") may give rise to self-mutilation in order to confirm being alive by feeling pain. Under such circumstances, the self-mutilation is often accompanied by fantasies in which the absent person is either believed to be performing the act or is being punished by the act.

The dynamics of self-destructive behaviors of borderline patients who are reacting to the absence of an important person are always complex and almost certainly involve several components. The components, however, are more purely intrapsychic than the interpersonal dynamics prevalent when the loss has not yet occurred. In the absence of this crucial person, latent convictions of innate badness may become overwhelming to some borderline patients.

The intrapsychic dynamics include: (1) efforts to remove or expel "badness" literally from one's body or self; (2) efforts to punish or hurt an internal "hated parent-image" who is experienced as overwhelming; or (3) an act of expiation for sins believed to have been committed toward a needed other. In this regard, patients may have borne a guilt for being alive, or the guilt may be related to having failed to cure the parent-therapist of some illness they feel responsible for causing. Finally, the behaviors can represent an altruistic retreat from externally directed anger, which serves as a private protest of one's innocence ("I wouldn't hurt anyone").

The degree to which these dynamics get concretized and internalized in bizarre forms reflects the degree to which the breakdown in reality testing has occurred and the degree to which the patient is attempting to deal with a state of intolerable aloneness. One patient, for example, believed that her slashing was "releasing the devil from my body." Another patient, in conscious emulation of his dead diabetic father, would slash himself "to feel as if I am with my father again." More typically, these dynamics do not take on such a concretized or explicitly distorted meaning, but are separated out into their various components only very gradually as part of an analysis of unconscious processes.

When Relationships Are Destroyed

There is a subgroup among borderline patients whose self-destructiveness represents a more malignant pattern. Self-destructiveness among this subgroup is identifiable by its relentlessness, urgency, and indiscriminate quality. When identified, the histories of such patients will often include extreme trauma, such as murders and suicides among close relatives during the patients' childhood development. The self-destructiveness is often a reaction to the permanent loss, usually by death, of a primary relationship.

Such patients generally require institutionalization, with sustained preventive restrictions. They usually need to form a strong institutional transference before they can respond to verbal psychotherapeutic limits or interpretative efforts. Such patients are the exception.

ASSESSMENT OF SELF-DESTRUCTIVE POTENTIAL

All of us who must evaluate the potential self-destructiveness of borderline patients need to distinguish between the relatively unusual suicide intent and the more common motives behind suicidal ideation. It is common and usually harmful to accept a patient's declaration of "feeling unsafe" as meaning he needs to be protected from suicidal options.

In our practice at McLean Hospital, we find it helpful to look at the interplay between the patient's emotional states and interpersonal relationships. What is the primary affect: depression, anger, or panic? Who is most important in the patient's life? Is that person present, frustrating, or absent? By answering these questions, the therapist will determine in a general sense how best to respond to threats of suicide. This is illustrated in Table 2.1. In addition, we should have answers to the following questions.

What is the patient's pattern of self-destructive behavior? How potentially lethal or serious has such behavior been in the past? What has been the interpersonal context of such behavior? How does the current situation resemble or differ from past situations? Evaluation of these questions can help to predict the borderline patient's self-destructive activity. This can then guide us to the most appropriate response.

CLINICAL MANAGEMENT

Most borderline patients undertake psychotherapy with only intermittent and adjunctive use of psychiatric hospitals, so the issue of a patient's ability to control self-destructive behavior or

Table 2.1
Core Affects and Responses

Affect	Key Person	Consequence	Therapist Response
Depressed	Present	Little risk of self-destructive acts	Proceed as usual
Angry	Frustrating	Interpersonally directed, self-destructive acts are common	Confrontation, clarification, interpretation
Panicked	Absent	Psychotic phenomena and intrapsychically motivated self-destructive acts are common	Unilateral active intervention

the degree of lethality involved—that is, the assessment of risk—will be in a "gray" zone where our clinical judgment is bound to be tested by the intrinsic uncertainties of the situation.

Borderline patients will frequently reveal their self-destructiveness in ways requiring concern and encouraging active noninterpretative interventions by therapists. A common example is when a patient misses an appointment after expressing suicidal impulses. Under such circumstances, a therapist is likely to feel that the patient is sadistically holding the "threat" of self-injury over the therapist's head. This is what has aptly been called "emotional blackmail." The therapist may refuse the manipulation and thereby risk the patient's physical welfare, or may comply with the manipulation and risk the patient's psychological growth. Neither of these approaches seems necessary or optimal. Instead, we believe that you can safely go along with the manipulation but only if the reason for the intervention is clarified, the meaning of the manipulation is interpreted, and the wisdom of both the patient's behavior and the therapist's responsiveness is explicitly questioned.

Examining the Risks of Active Interventions

It may make sense early in treatment for a therapist to telephone to inquire about a patient's missed appointments. Likewise, it may be natural to respond to a patient who complains of an untreated illness by urging medical care or to one who reports driving too rapidly by expressing concern. However, such commonplace indications of concern may lead to unwanted consequences. The borderline patient may voluntarily give up other functions or may expand the self-endangering behaviors with a new motive: to invite and test a therapist's apparent willingness to look out for the patient's best interests instead of having the patient do so.

The skill with which the therapist meets this problem will often determine whether and how quickly a safe and useful therapeutic process will occur. The following case illustrates a typical sequence of consequences that unsolicited interventions may have.

JENNIFER

Soon after Jennifer entered treatment because of a depression that led her to overdose, she reported to her therapist that she had a shard of glass in her foot that was festering. The doctor inquired about its severity and then suggested that she should have it seen by a physician. Jennifer seemed pleased by this unsolicited advice, but she missed her next appointment.

The therapist, worried, called, and she said she was unable to walk and no, she didn't go to see a doctor about her foot. The therapist replied that her wound could be quite dangerous and urged her to go to an emergency room and reminded her that their next appointment was in two days. She thanked him for calling and sadly added that the wound and her fever had conspired to make attending her recently acquired job impossible. Finally, she stated that she felt increasingly hopeless and depressed. The therapist inquired whether she felt suicidal. She replied she "didn't think so." He suggested an additional appointment. She agreed but did not appear at the appointed hour. After twenty minutes, her therapist overcame an angry impulse not to call because he feared that she might have over-dosed again—as she had the last time she'd described herself as "depressed." He called. There was no answer. Now he was really frightened. As he frantically searched for a phone number of some-one in the patient's family, she walked into his office looking very well.

By virtue of subtle but relentless evidence of self-destructiveness, a transition had occurred in this therapy in which the therapist gradually assumed increasing responsibility for the patient's well-being. The patient seemed to accept this passively. Because of the intense feelings generated in us as therapists, such a sequence often is the forerunner to the angry disruptions that lead to breaking off treatment and that unreasonably have given bor-derline patients such a bad name. This is unreasonable, since we must share the responsibility for this sequence when it occurs.

Avoiding Manipulation

In fact, borderline patients rarely ask explicitly for the interven-tions that are made on their behalf. Consequently we have little reason to be surprised when our unilateral efforts lead to regres-sions or accusatory flight rather than to the compliant gratitude we may expect. There is also little reason for a therapist to with-hold such interventions as long as it is made clear that the patient has actually asked for them. Once the patient's responsibility has been made clear, the desired sense of "magical control" is no longer at issue, and the patient will find little reason to continue the manipulation.

The benefits of insisting that borderline patients take respon-sibility for the interventions that they indirectly solicit is illus-trated in the case that follows.

CLAIRE

Near the end of a psychotherapy session in the hospital, Claire told her therapist that she had lost her appetite and that, in the past, this symptom had preceded her self-inflicted burns. The therapist inquired whether she was concerned that this might occur again. She said she didn't know. He asked whether she had informed the nursing staff. She replied she hadn't and that she didn't feel she could. The therapist expressed skepticism about this but asked whether she wanted him to do this for her. She didn't respond. Since the time was up, the therapist said he would be willing to talk with the nursing staff, but he wanted her to accompany him.

As they approached the nursing office, the patient became embarrassed by what was an increasingly obvious charade. In the nurses' presence, the therapist again inquired whether the patient wished him to speak for her. She angrily stalked off. The therapist told the nurse of the patient's symptom, the nursing staff responded with concern, and the exchange became the subject of subsequent psychotherapy sessions. The patient said she felt like a "baby" and resented that the therapist didn't "just do it" without "including her." The episode proved a useful frame of reference for understanding and circumventing the acting out of the patient's recurrent and highly charged passive controlling wishes; it also helped to illustrate the boundaries and functions of the psychotherapy.

In our practice, when we feel that a patient is "asking" indirectly for something, we try to point this out before intervening and inquire whether this perception is correct and what, if anything, the patient has in mind. When we feel we must undertake such supportive interventions without explicit solicitation, the patient's reaction to our intervention is explored immediately thereafter.

Some borderline patients will be surprised by the intervention. Its main significance may then be to invest the therapist with a transference as a primary object. Often borderline patients will say they felt the interventions were unnecessary or undesirable. We can then feel relieved of responsibility to continue what might otherwise become a progressive pattern. Having shown a willingness to act in response to what is felt to be indirect solicitation, we can safely discontinue this pattern of intervention only in response to a borderline patient's direct and explicit protest or after sufficient exploration has occurred in which the patient has come to recognize that it is not in his best interest for his therapist to continue to respond in that way. This often means that we must convey an inability to function as a therapist if the patient cannot work to understand his self-destructiveness without acting it out.

Avoiding Fatalities

If adequate investigation into the patient's reaction to our interventions is not undertaken, the provocative signals of impending self-destructive activity will recur and the danger to the patient will be even greater should we (or another involved party) fail to respond on cue. A fatal incident, like the following, may occur.

PAULA

Paula periodically rented a motel room and, with a stockpile of pills nearby, called her therapist's home with an urgent message. He responded by engaging in long conversations in which he "talked her down." Even as he told her that she could not count on his always being available, he became more wary of going out evenings without detailed instructions about how he could be reached. One night the patient couldn't reach him due to a bad phone connection. She fatally overdosed from what was probably a miscalculated manipulation.

Problems arise when a therapist, having offered supportive interventions, fails to inquire about or respect the patient's reactions to such interventions, assuming only that it gratifies the patient. In the example of Paula, the therapist had come to feel responsible for the patient's life and was increasingly involved in activity outside the psychotherapeutic arena. It is too simple to say that this is countertransference; it begins as a generally reasonable approach that will usually be useful with depressed patients. With borderline patients, however, the line between showing concern and inviting a regressive transference reaction is especially thin. The efforts to be supportive and available in Paula's case led to a progressive shift of responsibility for the patient's welfare onto the therapist. The therapist saw this shift as manipulative but also believed it to be warranted by the patient's neediness.

Supportive interventions bring about loss of function or increasing self-destructiveness when they are not accompanied by concurrent recognition and interpretation of the active, adaptive, and purposeful functions served by the patient's response to such interventions. Therapists are often aware only that such supportive work gratifies the patient's wish to be important to the therapist and to exercise control over her. Less obvious but essential for us to realize is that the borderline patient is also reacting to the frightening aspects of the therapist's growing invasiveness. In other words, the borderline patient can easily fear that he will be overwhelmed or controlled.

In the examples of both Jennifer and Paula, the therapist's supportive efforts needn't have led to further acting out by the patient—nor to as much anxiety for himself—had the oppositional, sadistic, and controlling nature of the patients' responses been anticipated, accepted, and interpreted.

In the case of Paula, an unworkable situation had developed. If a patient is unable to survive between appointments without repeated contacts with a therapist, hospitalization is indicated. In any event, such phone contacts should be focused on why the patient called and what is wanted: "I know you feel lousy, but what did you hope I could do for you?" This approach—without support or interpretation—will usually discourage the continuation of such phoning because it requires that the patients act collaboratively and make explicit what they can only hope to preserve by its remaining covert.

Acknowledging the Risks of Nonintervention

Thus far we've focused on issues that arise when a therapist intervenes supportively to prevent self-destructive behaviors. Equally common and perhaps more counterproductive is to minimize or ignore the self-destructive dangers. This can be due to a determinedly "analytic" stance by the therapist, or because the behaviors do not seem sufficiently dangerous, or because of a refusal to be manipulated. Whatever the reason, this reaction will encourage the patient to feel neglected or disliked, and borderline patients will respond by "testing" this—usually by flagrantly repeating or expanding their self-destructive behaviors, as illustrated in the next case.

LAURA

Laura moved to a new city and began outpatient therapy. After her second appointment, she called the therapist and reported that she had a knife and felt tempted to stab herself. In an ensuing session, she refused the therapist's recommendation to enter the hospital and noted that she was successfully finding an apartment and job. They agreed to meet more intensively for a while.

During the next week she became increasingly angry at the therapist for not giving her adequate direction and alluded again to recurrent impulses to stab herself. The therapist was determined to resist the unwanted burden of being responsible for the patient's life and to create a more "realistic" therapeutic climate. At the same time, he was increasingly concerned about the patient's safety. The issues reached a head when after leaving the therapist's office, she drove her car into a tree on the hospital grounds—literally outside his office window.

The therapist was shaken by the accident and angry at being forced to assume responsibility for her life. Her self-destructiveness had reached a point where it clearly was life endangering, and he decided he must insist on her admission. He recognized that she would respond angrily to this, but his major concern was that she would also find it a gratifying precedent.

In seeing her shortly after the car accident, he arranged for security people to assist in the hospitalization he was going to impose. He informed her of this intent but also informed her that it was not in her interest for him to decide how she should run her life and that she had forced him to do this. The patient responded by smashing his office and then curling up in a fetal position in the corner until she was bodily escorted to an inpatient service. The therapist later felt she had responded violently because she interpreted his statement as meaning that he didn't care about her. She later said she got enraged because he had security guards outside the office and that she would have entered the hospital cooperatively if he had "told" her to. In the course of the hospitalization, the patient decided to move back to a more familiar environment.

One of the important issues illustrated in this case is that therapists need to create situations in which their own anxiety can be sufficiently limited in order to help patients understand their behavior. In the first visit after she had called him about her suicidal impulses, the therapist should have stated that even if she opposed hospitalization, his own anxiety about her welfare was sufficient that it endangered his ability to function as a therapist for her. In this instance, both the immediate danger to the patient's safety and the dangers to the therapist's own well-being (legal, professional, and level of anxiety) necessitated the hospitalization.

The therapist underestimated the first issue (the danger to the patient) largely because he was fearful of overestimating the second issue; that is, he felt he shouldn't "give in" to the patient for reasons of his own well-being. Although it is clear, in retrospect, that his efforts to maintain his therapeutic neutrality in the course of hospitalizing her may have been ill timed, it is important in working with self-destructive borderline patients to convey that you are, in the long run, not able to take responsibility for their lives, that you are motivated by self-interest as well as by their interests, and that if they wish to know whether you or anyone cares about them, this cannot be learned by eliciting preventive responses to their self-destructiveness.

In this area in particular, we are governed by rules of conduct as professionals with legal responsibilities and by rules of society that require us to respond and that clearly complicate any interpretation of such "saving" responses as being motivated only by concern for a patient's welfare. The failure to clarify how social and legal obligations influence our interventions will encourage the repetition of the self-destructiveness.

Respecting the Responsible Adult in Your Patient

Defining the boundaries of the therapist's responsibilities and willingness to accept self-destructive behaviors emerges as a critical issue in the early phases of any intensive therapy with borderline patients. The pace was accelerated in Laura's case by the absence of any other people in her life. Within this vignette, we see the therapist vacillating between the two reactions commonly prescribed for borderline patients: "set limits, don't be manipulated"; and "be available, prevent suicide." These reactions are basically flip sides of the same coin in which the patient is being seen, unreasonably, either as an angry and greedy child or as a despairing waif.

Therapists easily overlook and fail to address the aspect of most borderline patients that genuinely wishes to use the therapist for constructive change. Indeed, treating the borderline patient as a potentially competent, responsible adult is one of the central tenets of the treatment philosophy termed "relationship management" by David Dawson and Harriet MacMillan. These psychiatrists from McMaster University describe the borderline patient's self-concept as a series of dichotomous positions including good versus bad, strong versus weak, competent versus incompetent, responsible versus not responsible, and in control versus not in control. They see this self-concept as context bound in that it shifts from one pole of these dichotomous positions to the other based on the interpersonal context. Thus, in a context in which they are seen as incompetent and not in control, as is the case far too often in their encounters with the mental health profession, borderline patients are likely to act incompetent and not in control. Conversely, if they are treated as competent adults who are in control, they are more likely to act that way.

Nevertheless, when patients seem to be seeking some form of supportive gratification, it is not obvious that they will be able to address the question of whether it is in their interests for you to deliver it—even if you could. The therapist in Laura's case was understandably uncomfortable about accepting a referral whom he experienced as immediately trying to place numerous unrealistic responsibilities on him. In this case, it is probably unreasonable to assign too much conscious manipulative intent to the patient. Thus, while it is important to keep in mind the tenets of relationship management, it is not always possible to follow them, as Laura's case illustrates.

Laura was desperate to find someone, anyone, to "hold on to," someone to feel in control of—an issue related to the third and lowest level of function, feeling interpersonally alone. Had the therapist recognized this, he would not have "personalized" her demands and perhaps would have been more appreciative of the need to help her arrange a more structured holding situation in her life—including the possibility of hospitalization—that would make psychotherapy possible. Because he felt that the patient was manipulating him into taking over responsibility by asking him for structure and was thus deflecting them from psychotherapeutic work, he underestimated her realistic needs.

THE USE OF MEDICATIONS

The use of medications in the management of patients with Borderline Personality Disorder has become commonplace over the past two decades. In many settings it is usual for medications to be prescribed by a psychiatrist while therapy is conducted by a nonmedical clinician. As it is not possible or desirable, from our point of view, to separate the issue of medications from the rest of the therapy, it is important for all involved treaters to be knowledgeable about the proper role and not insubstantial risks of pharmacotherapy in this patient population.

Virtually every class of psychotropic medication, including antidepressants, antipsychotics, anticonvulsants, lithium, anxiolytics, and opioid antagonists, has been advocated by one study or another. The plethora of pharmacological approaches speaks to both the varied and complex array of symptoms presented by the borderline patient and the relative ineffectiveness of any one type of medication. Because of the risks that borderline patients will misuse or overdose on prescriptions, the treaters need to be especially careful. A few general principles may prove helpful in diminishing such risks.

1. *Do no harm.* The medication prescribed to alleviate suffering can easily become the means of attempted suicide—manipulative, impulsive, or otherwise. This is not to say that the threat of suicide should dissuade you from providing a potentially helpful treatment but that the risks of overdose should be considered and discussed with the patient (see number four in this list) when deciding on the type and amount of medication prescribed. We feel that the therapist, even if not the prescribing doctor, needs to take an active role in this discussion, as the risk of misuse of medications is best seen in the broader picture of potentially self-destructive acts, and the therapist often has the best perspective on this picture.

2. *Be realistic.* Medications have never cured Borderline Personality Disorder. They are often modestly effective at treating co-morbid conditions like Major Depression and Panic Disor-

der, but are less helpful in alleviating some of the core symptoms of Borderline Personality Disorder such as feelings of emptiness and intolerance of aloneness. It is important for us not only to acknowledge this but also to convey it to our patients. When things get rocky, it can be tempting for us or our patients to conclude that "the meds aren't working." While this may well be true, it is at best a half-truth and at worst a dangerous deception.

Pinning unrealistically high hopes on medications and the search for the "right" pill frequently leads to repeated disappointment and a sense of failure, feelings all too common in the lives of these patients. In addition, patients may be reluctant to engage fully in the often long and painful work of therapy when they believe that a relatively quick and painless solution lies in a medicine bottle—if they could only find the right bottle. The feelings of hopelessness and aloneness that can be generated in these situations can lead to serious self-destructive acts.

3. Remember the dynamics. Medication can have many meanings for the borderline patient, but it is never without significance. On the one hand, medication may be seen as a wonderful gift, an expression of caring and nurturance in an otherwise hostile and unfeeling world. On the other hand, it may be seen as an unwanted, intrusive ploy by a domineering doctor to assert control. Negative feelings about medications can lead both to noncompliance, with resultant worsening of symptoms and increased risk of self-destructive activities, and to overdose— whether out of anger at the doctor, despair at the ineffectiveness of the treatment, or in an attempt to reassert control.

Before the patient begins medications, it is important to inquire about his feelings toward medication and to reassess them throughout the treatment as one would symptoms and side effects. Again, the therapist, who knows the patient best, should play a key role in this ongoing assessment.

4. Involve the patient. For the borderline patient this requires much more than a standard discussion of risks and benefits. Active participation by the patient in decision making must be insisted on. In addition to the benefits to be derived in a general sense from treating the patient as an autonomous responsible adult, insisting that the patient decide, and not merely consent, to take medication greatly diminishes the gratification to be derived from overdosing on "the doctor's" medication.

THE USE OF HOSPITALIZATION

The use of hospitalization is a common problem for therapists intent on not gratifying borderline patients' regressive wishes. Such therapists often view hospitals as harmfully regressive and either openly resist their use or openly encourage rapid discharge. We believe that such attitudes are likely to reinforce some borderline patients' paranoid fears of hospitals or to shame others who feel depressed into even more self-accusatory preoccupations.

To outpatients, a therapist's reluctance to use hospitals may convey a commitment to be with the patient even though this involves a course that could be life endangering. Instead, we believe that the therapist should make clear to the patient that she will at times exercise her independent judgment as to whether hospitalization is in the patient's best interests. This position can provide a reassuring structure or boundary within which the therapy takes place—and this, in turn, makes hospitalization far less likely.

To take a "limit-setting" position with borderline patients about hospitalizations will encourage a regressive transference characterized by the patient functioning at a lower level. Paradoxically, its effect is the same as taking the stance that the therapist is determined to prevent suicide. In the earlier example, Laura quickly recognized her therapist's countertransference concern about taking "too much" responsibility. It angered her that she was seen as "too much" and frightened her since she had no one else to whom she could turn. So she turned her car into the tree and eventually, on leaving the hospital, turned back to the world from which she came, with, we would guess, a deeper conviction of her inability to get something good from relationships.

This result is frequent when a therapist takes an approach that is openly wary of the patient's infantile gratifications. We believe that the therapists who advocate such an approach must only see those with whom such limits can be accommodated. Such patients usually do not form a deep transference relationship—which suits the therapist fine—and they are likely to use the therapist supportively even while they exercise their peculiar "behavioral specialty" on somebody outside the therapeutic arena. In such cases, the therapist's task often involves anticipating or interpreting the patient's self-destructive reactions to the vicissitudes of those relationships. Thus, hospitalization is something that some patients will occasionally require. We are as concerned about the effects on our patients of underuse of hospitalization as a treatment option as we are about the effects of its overuse.

Maintaining the Proper Balance

In this chapter we have documented the varied forms of serious self-destructive behavior characteristic of borderline patients. We want to emphasize again the importance of identifying whether such behaviors are primarily designed to (1) reassert a sense of control over some already established relationship, (2) locate and control a new person, or (3) delineate or destroy the patient's "bad" self.

We find that the first variation is the most common and the most problematic; the other variations, once identified, may require active unilateral interventions, but the gratifying aspects of these interventions are less central to the reason behind the act itself and thus are less likely to exacerbate the self-destructiveness. Keep in mind, however, that when such interventions are employed for the borderline patient who lacks a sustaining relationship, they serve to invest the therapist with those sustaining functions. Thereafter the therapist may become the target for the first type of self-destructive behaviors (that is, the manipulative ones), which are designed to elicit some saving response. If such a saving response is again elicited, it will be likely to perpetuate the self-destructiveness.

Recognition of this problem has been the usual rationale for a limit-setting approach. We have observed that such a limit-setting approach can also result in further and more dangerous self-destructiveness because it can heighten the borderline patient's sense of rejection and aloneness and thereby transform what was originally an interpersonal manipulation into the more dangerous private act of self-delineation or self-destruction.

As Otto Kernberg has described, the problem is how to provide sufficient support or structure so that a psychotherapy can take place without foregoing the therapist's essential neutrality in the process. Therapists who become intent on preserving their neutrality or who are highly resistant to taking responsibility away from a patient are likely to give inadequate support when it is needed and to exaggerate the power of transference interpretations directed toward manipulation at times when the patient's self-destructive behaviors are due to the absence of a crucial relationship.

We believe that the tensions surrounding self-endangering activity can be resolved by a therapist's readiness to be manipulated as long as the saving response is accompanied by clarification and analysis of its meaning. This includes an early clarification, on the therapist's part, of her limited ability to prevent suicide and of her legal obligation to intervene and its possible effect of therapy. And it involves early clarification of the harmful and potentially irreconcilable effects that the need for any lifesaving activity will have on the therapist's ability to function and on the patient's ability to have a useful therapeutic experience. It has been our experience that the consistent, firm, clear, and sometimes repetitious description of these parameters provides a reassuring boundary that most borderline patients will recognize and even appreciate.

One of the major problems therapists have occurs when they provide supportive interventions without interpretation of the hostile and controlling motivations of patients or when they fail to recognize and respect that such interventions have frightening as well as gratifying significance. A second major problem therapists have is that their concerns about preserving technical neutrality and insisting on collaboration will lead them to personalize too much and fail to intervene in self-destructive activity not primarily designed to manipulate them but reflecting the degree to which a patient's primary supports elsewhere in his life are failing him.

We hope that this chapter has shed light on some of the more troubling and challenging aspects of the care of borderline patients. We encourage you to draw from our experience, and we expect that soon the term *borderline* will evoke a reaction of ardor rather than dread.

NOTES

P. 25, *"behavioral specialty"*: Mack, J. (1975). Borderline states: An historical perspective. In Mack, J. (Ed.), *Borderline States in Psychiatry* (pp. 20–35). New York: Grune & Stratton.

P. 26, *study conducted at McLean Hospital*: Gunderson, J., Kolb, J., & Austin, V. (1981). The diagnostic interview for borderline patients. *American Journal of Psychiatry, 138*, 896–903.

P. 28, *lifetime prevalence of completed suicide*: Stone, M. H., Hunt, S. W., & Stone, D. K. (1987). The PI 500: Long-term follow-up of borderline inpatients meeting *DSM-III* criteria: 1. Global outcome. *Journal of Personality Disorders, 1*, 291–298; Paris, J., Howles, D., Brown, R. (1987). Long-term follow-up of borderline patients in a general hospital. *Comprehensive Psychiatry, 28*, 530–535.

P. 28, *study at McLean Hospital*: Sabo, A. N., Gunderson, J. G., Najavits, L. M., Chauncey, B., & Kisiel, C. (1995). Changes in self-destructiveness of borderline patients in psychotherapy: A prospective follow-up. *Journal of Nervous and Mental Disease, 183*(6), 370–376.

P. 30, *manipulative manner*: Sifneos, P. (1966). Manipulative suicide. *Psychiatric Quarterly, 40*, 525–537.

P. 31, *intolerable states of aloneness:* Adler, G., & Buie, D. (1979). Aloneness and borderline psychopathology: The possible relevance of child development issues. *International Journal of Psychoanalysis, 60,* 83–96.

P. 32, *"hated parent-image":* Searles, H. (1980, April). *Psychoanalytic therapy with borderline patients: the development in the patient of an internalized image of the therapist.* Paper presented at the fifth O. Spurgeon English Honor Lecture at Temple University School of Medicine, Philadelphia.

P. 34, *"emotional blackmail":* Brenman, M. (1952). On teasing and being teased and the problem of moral masochism. *The Psychoanalytical Study of the Child, 7,* 264–285.

P. 42, *"relationship management":* Dawson, D., & MacMillan, H. (1993). *Relationship management of the borderline patient: From understanding to treatment.* New York: Brunner/Mazel.

P. 48, *how to provide sufficient support or structure:* Kernberg, O. (1975). *Borderline conditions and pathological narcissism.* New York: Jason Aronson.

CHAPTER

3

COMBINED TREATMENT APPROACH WITH BORDERLINE PATIENTS

Alan Bardikoff

Therapists working with borderline patients often find themselves struggling at different points in the therapeutic process with difficulties that are unlike the challenges they face with their other patients. These difficulties present themselves in various ways and can sometimes force the therapy to a crisis point; then, unless the crisis is handled properly, treatment may be severely compromised or terminated. Such conflictual components, while a part of all therapeutic alliances, are nonetheless so characteristic of work with borderlines that they have become a hallmark of these particular patients' course of treatment.

I have found that a treatment approach that considers various options for addressing the borderline's needs will be most effective in responding to daily pressures experienced by the patient, as well as in reducing both the individual's and the therapist's reactions to the therapeutic process. This chapter will present the reasons for a combined treatment approach, as well as discuss some of the options available and when they might best be considered.

SPECIAL DIFFICULTIES WITH BORDERLINE PATIENTS

The question of why therapeutic work with the patient with Borderline Personality Disorder (BPD) is so difficult can be examined from several different viewpoints.

A Lack of Cohesive Self

Some therapists see the problems in treatment with these patients as reflecting the patient's deficient intrapsychic structures. A lack of cohesive sense of self leaves the BPD patient unable to establish and maintain close relationships based on a shared understanding of mutual respect and commitment.

As a result, such patients need to paralyze the treatment process because of the fragmented and confused feelings they experience when the therapist attempts to establish some sense of a relationship. For these patients the experience of having someone close and involved deeply in their lives prompts regression and rekindles past losses. Good therapeutic work, therefore, is felt by the patient to be intrusive and threatening, as it stimulates long-held disappointments that blend all experiences and relationships into one great pool of regret. Consequently, the borderline patient is difficult to treat because the nature of the therapeutic process presents challenges and conflicts that prevent, at least initially, the establishment of a therapeutic alliance.

Overemphasis on the Theory of Development

A second perspective on the difficulties that arise in treating borderlines focuses on the theoretical approaches used to explain and understand these patients. Here the conflicts and difficulties are perceived as reflecting problems in the therapist's understanding of the patient's true needs. A focus on the theory of development—on innate aggression, or drives—serves to distance the therapist from the patient's true experience and can result in additional injuries and insults to a person already hyper-sensitive to being misunderstood.

Such failures in empathic attunement are the result of incor-rect therapeutic practice, for in looking for the theory within the individual's presentation, the therapist has ignored or devalued the patient's feelings within their relationship. The result for the borderline patient is an estrangement and disappointment with therapy similar to that experienced with other forms of human interaction where the patient has felt dissatisfied and unfulfilled.

Reciprocal Components

A third perspective focuses on the interaction between the intrapsychic needs of both the patient and the therapist. In this approach it is the reciprocal components of the therapeutic process that cause the greatest challenge to treating the border-line patient. Acknowledging that we therapists also enter the therapeutic process with needs left unmet, this perspective asks that we recognize the powerful influence the patient's needs and feelings can have on our thoughts. When these feelings become too powerful and require too much of our attention, the thera-pist's struggle to contain and understand his own feelings com-promises the therapeutic process and again leaves the patient feeling alone, abandoned, and hopeless.

Regardless of the perspective one wishes to adopt in conceptu-alizing work with the BPD patient, there is hardly any disagree-ment about the pressure this work places on the therapist. The therapist and the patient are often joined in their profound dis-satisfaction with the course of treatment, and both experience interventions as unsatisfactory and disappointing. The comple-mentarity of their experience leaves both feeling as if they are on a treadmill, continually expending energy to go over the same ground yet ultimately feeling as if they end at the same place that they began.

A LOOK AT THE OPTIONS

Each of the perspectives just outlined can be useful in structuring treatment with a BPD patient. It is safe to say, however, that no one perspective will work for each patient and that the choice of approach should probably reflect the patient's needs and circumstances, as well as her past treatment history. In addition, factors influencing the delivery of care are also a component in this equation, as the therapist needs to be clear just how much service will be available for the patient and how these concerns will shape treatment.

Just as no one theoretical perspective will address all BPD patients, so too no one clinical perspective will meet all the challenges posed by this diagnostic group. Understanding borderline patients' needs requires that we recognize that their treatment must involve more than facilitating the process of gaining insight and awareness about defenses or unsatisfied self needs. Work with borderline patients challenges the therapist to expand the therapeutic structure and to work with a multitude of options and approaches that will respond to the practical elements that these patients have to address in the course of reorganizing their life.

In this chapter we will first consider *why* one might need to explore alternative approaches in work with borderline patients. Here we will discuss the therapist's feelings and how these need to be addressed in order for the complicated and sometimes confusing work with the borderline patient to be understood and responded to therapeutically. Some of these reactions include feelings of being overwhelmed by the patient, difficulties with the affective disruptions that characterize these patients' lives, and dependency concerns.

Following this we will explore *when* it may be necessary to consider options to complement or substitute for individual psychotherapy with the borderline patient. Here we will focus on both the patient's and the therapist's reactions to the treatment process and how these reactions can help in determining a proper course of action.

Examples of some of the problems and pressures that may prompt consideration of supportive auxiliary measures include excessive worry about the patient's self-harm potential; anger with the patient's inability to remain consistent in the therapeutic process; and exhaustion and resentment at the demands made by the patient for the therapist's time and attention.

Closely related to the discussion of when one considers a shift in treatment structure with a borderline patient is the question of *how* one reflects on the process of treatment and then plans for a desired change. In this section we will focus on clinical consultation and how one uses this resource in reviewing treatment objectives and progress. The clinical case presented will share both the feelings and the content of the consultation process and illustrate how treatment was reorganized as a result.

The concluding section of the chapter will present *what* options exist for the therapist to consider for the borderline patient. These options include family therapy, group psychotherapy, social skills training, inpatient hospital and day treatment programs, and rehab and job-training programs.

The linear presentation of this chapter may seem to imply that work with the borderline patient begins as individual psychotherapy and then proceeds to a multimodal approach when either party feels overwhelmed or dissatisfied with the process. This, however, is not the case. I have found that an assessment of the structure of treatment happens at many points and under different circumstances reflecting each patient's situation and needs. Borderline patients are often referred for psychotherapy following crises or hospitalizations, when there is already a treatment component in place that may or may not be useful as an ongoing resource. Since we learn the most about patients through the establishment of a relationship, we must recognize that it is only through the process of assessment and treatment that we can understand how best to address a patient's needs. The process of reviewing and establishing a treatment plan can, therefore, happen at numerous points in time and at different places along the continuum of the why, when, how, and what dimensions presented here.

WHY A COMBINED TREATMENT APPROACH IS NEEDED

The reasons for proceeding with a combined treatment approach may be best understood when we consider the feelings evoked in both the therapist and the patient by the treatment process. Establishing a therapeutic relationship with the BPD patient presents unique emotional difficulties for the patient that often argue against the intensity of a one-to-one psychotherapeutic approach. For many of these patients, the regression that results from the dependency they feel is too great to assimilate while still maintaining normal functioning.

The process of creating and then functioning within such a troubled relationship can present unique emotional difficulties for the therapist as well. The struggle to maintain a balance among the feelings discussed in therapy, the pressures faced by these patients in their everyday lives, and one's own reactions to the feelings in the room can be demoralizing, frustrating, frightening, and depressing, to name but a few of the feelings experienced and written about by therapists. These pressures and the problems they represent are the first focus of this chapter.

Features of the Therapeutic Alliance

For the therapist, dealing with a patient's anger, loneliness, sadness, and even hopelessness is far from an unusual experience, as most people seek out treatment because of such feelings. With the borderline patient, however, what is often absent from the therapeutic process is a sense that the discussion of events is taking place within the context of a relationship based on continuity and consistency, predictability and empathy. In these situations, it is often extremely difficult to feel confident as a therapist in one's judgment about the relationship and the patient's ability to use insights gained through the relationship in the management of daily demands. Will the patient be able to hear and use the intervention? Should one in fact be making an interpretation at this point? But if one doesn't and things go wrong, will the patient harm herself? Will she be able to continue in treatment if she feels her therapist has "failed" her?

The challenges these difficult patients present are often felt by the therapist as personal and reflective of some sort of failure or limitation in the therapist's ability to be empathic or knowledgeable in structuring treatment. While the devaluing process may be something the therapist is aware of from training or previous cases, the experience of being caught within this web of needs, defenses, and feelings can be quite profound. Therapists can feel overwhelmed by their borderline patients and the apparent uselessness of treatment in improving their daily lives. The therapist may also feel the tremendous weight of the patient's pain and suffering, as the patient continues to unload and deposit these feelings in the therapeutic sessions. The borderline patient may also devalue the therapist, criticizing weaknesses observed and errors made or perceived. These kinds of attacks make it difficult to remain connected to the patient's overriding feelings of despondency, isolation, and loneliness.

The Need for a Therapeutic Shift

The following two-part vignette illustrates the difficulties of working with a BPD patient. The first section presents the earlier part of the case when the therapist was overwhelmed by the complex feelings the patient had evoked in him. These feelings prevented him from responding optimally to the patient. The therapist was also unable to adapt and change the process of interaction to offer a different experience for the patient in their relationship.

In the second section, treatment proceeds more effectively as the therapist adjusts his approach to respond to both the patient's reactions to the therapeutic experience and to the major pressures she was complaining about in her life.

VIVIAN

Vivian, thirty-four, entered therapy requesting help in her relationships with men and in parenting her ten-year-old son, Ryan. Vivian's borderline features included a fierce temper that she would demonstrate at unpredictable times when her son Ryan had angered her. Her relationships with men, and in fact with anyone who got close to her, had all ended in failure, a pattern she was aware of but unable really to examine. Wildly enthusiastic as a relationship would begin, she would gradually become angry and disappointed by her boyfriends, then sullen and morose as it became clear to her that this relationship was not the right one. Ryan's needs were always a complicating factor, and she would become furious with him as the competing claims made by her son and her boyfriend would grow intolerable.

Vivian worked as a sales representative for a large firm where she appeared to be excelling. Her work required her to leave her home at 6:30 each morning, returning home around dinnertime. Children's Aid had been alerted by the school prior to my involvement because of the long periods of time when the child had minimal supervision. Ryan, who was presenting with behavior problems at school and at home, was seen as a child with a growing willingness to challenge authority figures.

Treatment began as one-to-one psychotherapy with the emphasis on understanding Vivian's feelings toward those close to her. The focus moved between Vivian's experience as a child and the discipline she received, and her reactions to Ryan's misbehavior and its consequences. As Ryan's behavior became more problematic, Vivian began to speak about the inadequacy of psychotherapy and her need for active support in managing Ryan's escalating behavior problems.

Efforts at helping Vivian recognize that her reactions to Ryan were similar to her feelings toward men and other people close to her in general were met with ridicule and anger. Exploring the anger and its relationship to her own upbringing brought on more rage and frustration with the therapeutic process. Continued attempts to help Vivian look at her role in Ryan's misbehavior did little to avert

her angry feelings with Ryan and with me and provoked stronger
feelings of panic and urgency in her need for relief. My concerns for
Ryan also became important, as Vivian's rage appeared frightening
in its intensity.

Despite efforts at establishing an effective framework in which
Vivian could respond to her feelings, I observed little progress.
I felt ineffective and unimportant in a situation in which Vivian
nevertheless turned to me in times of crisis or strain. As Vivian's
frustration with her son grew, her willingness to examine her
behavior and the repetitive patterns of relationships with men—
husband, boyfriends, father, therapist, and son—disappeared, and
the focus shifted to her desperate attempt to control Ryan and
his behavior. Even though I could plainly see the connections
between Vivian's current struggles with her son and these past
problems, the issue was no longer available for consideration by
the client. The change in Vivian's goals, a reaction to numerous
influences, left me unable to pursue the earlier plan we had
agreed on. A shift needed to occur in treatment in order for me
to "catch up" to the patient's new definition of why she was in
therapy.

When Ryan stole from her and a neighbor, Vivian poured out a
tirade of vindictiveness and accusation that was overwhelming in its
intensity. She could not be moved from her insistence that Ryan had
to get "straightened out." Feeling that these pressures had to be
addressed, I recommended that Vivian bring Ryan to my office for
family sessions to discuss the problems observed at home and at
school. At that point, family therapy became the primary treatment
focus, with both structural and strategic suggestions and interventions forming the basis of the work.

A consultation session with school personnel was organized in
my office to discuss Ryan's progress and needs. Vivian appeared

motivated and eager to work on the relationship with her son and establish a new balance between them that had her firmly enforcing an agreed-on structure. A referral for a Big Brother was made and eventually followed through. A definite improvement was noted in Ryan's behavior at school and in the community. Vivian, while still very upset by the challenges she experienced at home, was nonetheless pleased about Ryan's more cooperative behavior and his willingness to make an effort at school.

As these issues faded into the background with the passage of time and some improvement on Ryan's part, Vivian would speak about how much she loved Ryan and wanted never to lose him. She would stress that they really had no one but themselves and therefore had to stick together.

The shift away from individual psychotherapy had clearly been needed in this case. The patient's sensitivity and mistrust of others became more and more pronounced as the relationship with me became established. The regression and its impact on the patient's functioning, the difficulty managing the patient's extreme reactions to the circumstances, and the pressing need to address Ryan's behavior and feelings argued for a family therapy approach. The shift to address the major issues in Vivian's life did not entirely lessen her frustration with me or her anger with everyone's failure to fix her child. It did, however, help her contain her feelings about being in a relationship with a therapist and provide her with a method of airing her irritations with her son. It also provided me with a method of monitoring Vivian's interaction with her child.

The Therapist's Reactions

Initially the therapist is often unsure what's going on and so feels the need to catch up with the patient and thereby reassert some sense of himself in the therapeutic process. In the case just described, confronting the patient with her style of managing crises had not met with any success and, in fact, had made things more difficult as Vivian responded to these interventions as attacks. However, it is also obvious that I felt devalued and unsure of myself in these interactions. Left feeling insecure and worried about Ryan and issues of child welfare and protection, I was absorbed into a system that operated in a crisis intervention mode, hastily moving from one fire to another, always too busy or preoccupied to stop and examine how the very system contributed to the difficulties encountered.

The therapist's feelings in this situation were tremendously important in understanding this woman and her needs. Unfortunately, the pressures of reacting and responding continually kept me off balance and unable to process my thinking and feeling about the patient's behavior. I could not deal with the fact that Vivian's initial interest in therapy was like her feelings about a new relationship, begun with excitement but soon to lose its luster as the process left her feeling disappointed and empty. I also couldn't work with my protectiveness toward Ryan because these feelings represented a betrayal of Vivian, a choice for her son and not her. Caught among all these conflicting feelings, I felt unable to use my insights or my experience without fearing the repercussions they would have on Ryan or on the process of therapy.

These experiences convey important information about what it is like to have a close relationship with Vivian. The discounted, confused, and devalued feelings I was experiencing are probably duplicates of some of Ryan's feelings, as he too struggles to feel valued and respected in his relationship with his mother. If I were to dismiss these feelings—avoiding them by terminating with the patient or allowing her to control the interaction—an opportunity would be missed to intervene meaningfully and informatively in their lives.

Questions of what represents the best you can do for a patient become extremely important as the therapist begins to reexamine and redefine the goals for this kind of therapeutic process. This can of course lead you to doing a different type of therapy than you usually do or than you thought you were going to do with this person at the beginning of treatment.

WHEN TO CONSIDER A COMBINED APPROACH

Determining when to suggest a shift in treatment focus depends on the therapist's assessment of two components of the therapeutic relationship: the patient's functioning and the therapist's feelings. They are far from independent or unrelated, but I will present them separately here to clarify when consideration of augmenting a treatment plan may be in order.

The Patient's Experience

In considering when to augment treatment with a BPD patient, the therapist must complement clinical judgment with careful attention to the concerns and comments voiced by the patient. Often the process of psychotherapy can be frustrating and upsetting for the BPD patient. A focus on internal need states and emotions may stand in opposition to the increasing need for practical strategies and solutions to pressing problems. The difficulties experienced by these patients in responding to the challenges of everyday life can easily override their earlier interest and intention to focus on the past and understand their emotions. Despite efforts by the therapist to empathize and interpret current crises in light of past events and the patient's sense of repetition, the BPD patient's pressure for help now can derail the psychotherapeutic process if it is not responded to appropriately.

In addition to listening to the patient's need for help with life's pressures, the therapist needs to be sensitive to the complaint and fear that no progress is being made. Whether this concern is voiced in the midst of a crisis in the patient's life or in response to some impasse in the therapeutic process, it represents a real and powerful expression of the BPD patient's difficulty with the process of therapy and, as such, must also be dealt with carefully.

It is not necessary to view these difficulties as failures of the process, the patient, or oneself. Accepting that our patients' needs change, we may be in a position to provide the BPD patient with a truly helpful experience in discussing the impasse. Helping frame an understanding of the need for change in terms of life's pressures and the challenge of taking slow and steady steps that reflect a realistic sense of the patient's world may provide the BPD with a feeling of success and accomplishment that might foster reflection and assist the patient in the future.

Listening to the patient's experience will also help in organizing a response to his regression in the face of the intense feelings evoked through treatment and the process of establishing some emotional closeness with the therapist. Often the failure to attend to these reactions in our patients can be at the root of their more negative and destructive behaviors. The patient's violent feelings, relentless attacks on the therapist, and the devaluing or avoidance may all represent the struggles the patient is experiencing in the face of establishing some sense of closeness with another individual. Sometimes these feelings are simply unavailable for examination in therapy, and it is important that the therapist understand and respect the BPD patient's need for distance and escape from the overwhelming feelings that accompany this process. Understanding when this is occurring for the patient is a central component of treatment with the BPD and a facet of the work that can be extremely significant in determining what to do next.

The Therapist's Experience

From the therapist's perspective, issues concerning the treatment of the BPD patient need to be understood as part of a process of ongoing assessment and reevaluation of treatment goals and patient needs. While we may find that with any patient, regardless of diagnosis, constant review and evaluation are occurring, with the BPD this process takes on a different tone precisely because of the difficulty gauging the impact of the relationship on the patient's functioning and the BPD patient's propensity to decompensate quickly in the face of certain challenges and feelings.

This can perhaps best be illustrated when one considers the affective disruptions observed in the work with borderline patients.

The process of creating a relationship often elicits profound regression in these patients as, in the midst of establishing what is so painfully absent in their lives, their unmet needs overwhelm them. At times when one might expect sadness or reflection, the patient may present with neither, expressing a cavalier or unconcerned pose that negates what the therapist had been expecting and fostering. Similarly, extreme anger and pain may also be expressed at junctures that appear somewhat innocuous or minor. These disruptions characterize work with the borderline patient and have a significant impact on the therapist's judgment about how to proceed.

In situations where self-harm is a feature, this confusion can also be potentially dangerous, as the therapist struggles with a lack of understanding about what is going on and what to do. Therapeutic interventions that in the past were comforting and containing are no longer helpful. Disruptions and challenges to the process are frequent, and the therapist may be unsure whether sessions with the patient will be supportive or will perhaps lead to further deterioration in the therapeutic alliance and regression in the patient's functioning.

Ongoing Assessment

The process of ongoing assessment of the patient may be best thought of as determining the needs of the patient along a continuum of levels ranging from acute, to rehabilitation, to maintenance. Each level has its own focus and treatment objectives and, by definition, changes the approach adopted by the therapist.

Acute care can be understood as immediate and substantial coverage and monitoring for a patient during a period of decompensation or potential self-harm.

Rehabilitation suggests an emphasis on a return to previous functioning levels, along with a sense of attempting to improve the patient's circumstances. And maintenance implies a need for preventing further decompensation and a maintaining of current achievement and comfort levels.

This kind of framework can prove useful for the therapist in adjusting treatment goals and objectives. Patients at the acute level will not be able to do the kind of psychotherapeutic work that a patient who feels safe and has no suicidal thoughts is capable of. Obviously patients at the rehabilitation level will see themselves as ready to work on their issues or at least ready to talk about them in a manner in which the acute-level patient is just not ready.

Perhaps more so than most other patients, the BPD patient presents with a changing picture of needs and symptoms. Thinking about the patient's needs in terms of a model like the simple one presented here will also help in considering the impact of Axis I features on the BPD patient's functioning. Often Axis I conditions are overlooked with the BPD patient because of the pervasiveness of their symptom presentation. However, the presence of these additional diagnoses have a definite impact on the kind of treatment offered, especially if the Axis I element is acute and the patient has no chronic history. These kinds of considerations become extremely important when considering self-harm and the potential risk a patient's behavior represents at the time.

Focusing on the assessment of patient needs also implies that you are aware of countertransference issues and reactions to the various stages and developments within treatment and how these may be influencing the process. These feelings are another barometer of the need for change in the treatment structure or focus. We mentioned earlier how difficult therapy with BPD patients can be in triggering the therapist's emotions and unresolved issues. Whether these result, for example, from the patient's dependency on the therapist, from the extreme anger and devaluing that can take place within the relationship, or even from the unending crisis that therapy seems to be with the BPD patient, they represent realities of the therapist's feelings and are, therefore, part of the process of treatment. It is when these feelings are out of control that the process of review and rethinking of needs and objectives must also take place.

As therapists, the time for change can be recognized when we find ourselves dreading our patient's sessions, fearful of what she may say or do, and unable to contain our worries within a reasonable framework. Aware that something needs to change within our understanding of the therapeutic relationship with the patient, we can now turn to the next section to examine how one reviews this work and determines where the process should go.

How to Review Treatment: The Consultation Process

A useful, perhaps even necessary adjunct to work with borderline patients is the consultative process in which the therapist is able to discuss and review treatment objectives with a colleague who can provide another perspective on the relationship between patient and therapist.

While considering consultation may appear simple, the feelings that mark the problems with the patient can often color the therapist's approach to the consultative process. In seeking support, the therapist may feel like a failure, embarrassed over his inability to manage the patient's needs, or upset at the outcome of a therapeutic process that has them both acting and thinking differently than they feel they would have in other situations.

The therapist may also feel angry at the patient's behavior and lack of proper appreciation for the relationship that has been so patiently fostered. This anger may be somewhat difficult to acknowledge.

As therapists we all know that we are supposed to be in control of these and other feelings in the therapeutic encounter. This control is supposed to allow us to focus all our thinking and feelings on the treatment process, without the troublesome component of our unchecked emotions. Having to admit to and identify the pressure that working with one of our borderline patients has exerted on our own needs and anxieties is not easy. No matter how much one speaks about the difficulty of working with the significant emotional pressures these patients exert, it is hard to interrupt the process and stop to examine oneself, especially if, as we have indicated, that process itself already has a sour taste to it.

Moving Toward Consultation

The following case provides a good example of the confused feelings one therapist brought to the consultation process.

LISA

Lisa, twenty-six, was diagnosed borderline even prior to being referred to me. She presented with an eating disorder, chronic anger and depression, and ineffective social and work relations despite being quite bright and educated. Married for three years, Lisa had never really separated from her mother. She still called her mother several times a day and spent all her free time with her, even though she professed to hate these obligations. Unable to say no, she would become increasingly anxious and angry as she prepared for the weekly shopping outings with her mother. Lisa had been obese in her childhood and early adolescence until shortly after her favored older sister had run away to get married. At that point she had stopped eating in an effort to guarantee herself a spot within her mother's highly critical view of the world. She had been hospitalized on two occasions for her eating disorder, once on a crisis basis.

Lisa's progress in therapy deteriorated over the course of six months as tensions between her husband and her mother intensified. Her mother owned the business that employed Lisa's husband and also provided her with a small wage for bookkeeping and computer services. Her anxiety and her anorexia had, however, prevented her from working for about the past year, and Lisa had come to feel unbearably controlled by her mother's power over her and the family.

As Lisa identified her desire to separate from her mother, she began to take steps to create some boundaries between them. The pressure of these steps prompted an increase in sessions to two times a week. Initially this appeared to provide the patient with some comfort and support, but as the pressure mounted on Lisa, it became apparent that cutting back the sessions was out of the question. Lisa's anxiety skyrocketed as her tentative steps to separate from her mother evoked a strong reaction from her mother that was both rejecting and punitive. Despite the support of her husband in these moves, Lisa felt vulnerable and alone and quickly regretted her actions. Her eating disorder became potentially more dangerous, and weekly monitoring with her family doctor was instituted.

An additional complication resulted after the patient was hospitalized for ten days with a medical problem unrelated to her anorexia or borderline symptomatology; her recuperation period of three weeks' bed rest prevented her from attending office appointments. Her fears and panic, however, were almost out of control at the time, and I agreed to a brief period of telephone sessions to bridge this difficult period. Again the sessions grew to twice weekly as the patient spoke about how no one really understood how alone she felt and how afraid she was at all times. The interruption of her life's routines created a major issue as the patient regressed and refused to venture outside the house without her husband. The patient also began to speak of her deepening depression and her feeling that if she didn't have a child she would find little reason left to live. Her response to my inquiries about suicidality were negative, but on several occasions her husband brought her to appointments or to the family doctor so that a mental status assessment could be properly conducted.

I felt unable to change the telephone sessions as the patient's anxiety and depression worsened at the thought of either venturing out on her own or discontinuing the contact. Medication had been prescribed by the family doctor, but it had brought little relief. The depression had deepened and telephone sessions were consumed with tearful pleas for some relief from the pain of her existence. Appointments would be scheduled in my office but Lisa would not show, sometimes calling in distress at the end of the day to explain that her car had broken down or her son was ill, and so on. The patient's need to be seen would result in visits to her general practitioner, who was concerned but did not see her as suicidal. Finally, an attempt was made by the emergency room staff to hospitalize Lisa, but it was a disaster, leaving the therapist and the hospital at odds about diagnosis and treatment. Feeling alone, confused, and somewhat mistreated by the hospital staff, I became very worried and anxious about where the case was heading. It was at this point that a consultation was requested.

Setting the Objectives

A careful conceptualization of the purpose of the consultation will help identify the value of the exercise and the areas of difficulty that the therapist is experiencing. Four particular features guide the request, each illustrating the opportunity that the consultation process offers for review and assistance.

First, the opportunity to review one's clinical work and examine a patient's progress can only be helpful. Discussing impressions and plans for the patient, reflecting on interventions and their purpose, and speculating on the change the therapist feels is evident comprise an extremely useful exercise. Doing these things with a colleague who will then meet with the patient provides an opportunity to challenge, rethink, and reorganize one's approach. Considering the multitude of problems Lisa presented with, I felt at the time of the consultation that any help was going to be appreciated.

The consultation process also assists the therapist by looking at the therapist's feelings about the course of treatment, especially the feeling of being caught providing a service that is feeding the patient's regression. The strength of this patient's dependency needs had become so great that I had become tentative and uncertain, assisting in crisis management but unable to move beyond these pressures to help effect some more meaningful change. Having the opportunity to vent and share this responsibility helped me begin to examine why this had occurred and how it could best be addressed in the context of the therapeutic relationship.

Consultation can also be used to explore some of the theoretical questions about the lack of a cohesive self and related impasses discussed earlier in this chapter. Effective treatment is only possible when there is an understanding of how to approach stalemates like the one described in Lisa's case. Is the problem a reflection of incorrect therapeutic interventions? Does it reflect the intrapsychic features of the patient? And what kind of intervention would be most helpful in the future? Could this patient benefit from insight-inspired interventions, or would she be best helped by supportive and practical interventions? While therapy might be composed of a mixture of these different approaches, what is the impact of choosing one focus over the other, and how will the therapist gauge this impact in the future?

And finally, are there other resources one could bring to the case that would augment the individual work and assist the patient in her progress outside the office? On an immediate basis, this may include medication needs and the establishment of a more effective treatment plan. On a longer-term basis, this may involve consideration of inpatient and day hospital admissions, group work, job retraining, and family therapy.

It would be encouraging to be able to say that after the consultation in Lisa's case, things went smoothly with no further problems or challenges. In fact this was only partially true. The opportunity to consult helped reorganize and reconceptualize the treatment plan. With the encouragement and involvement of the consultant, the therapist was able to set an acceptable time frame with the patient for the conclusion of the telephone sessions. A somewhat better medication plan was developed. And as a result of the emphasis on reviewing and evaluating the course of treatment, the patient and the therapist decided on a target date for gradually increasing her activity levels outside the house. While far from problem free, the patient did begin a day hospital program and then a job readiness program, both of which were perceived by her as helpful and positive developments in her life.

The consultation was also valuable for the therapist. In addition to helping clarify a treatment plan for the patient, the process allowed the therapist to explore both the feelings and the events that had resulted in the circumstances described in the case study. As a contribution to ongoing learning about the needs of the BPD and of the therapist, it was invaluable.

What Are the Treatment Options to Consider?

The various options available to the therapist in considering how best to respond to the BPD patient will obviously depend on resources within a particular community and the treatment history of the patient. In this section we will focus on three options—hospitalization, group therapy, and family or marital therapy—though others are certainly available and may deserve attention. The following case study will provide an introduction to this subject.

A Crucial Collaboration

EVELYN

Evelyn, twenty-six and married for seven years to Mark, twenty-eight, was being seen in therapy for problems in her relationships at work and with family members. Her presentation included a serious eating disorder, anxiety and panic in social situations, numerous somatic complaints, and a tremendous fear of being abandoned by her spouse. This fear of abandonment had been explored in conjoint sessions with only mild success, despite the fact that Mark had worked hard at assuring her of his love.

Mark had even attended a consultation session on his own, following Evelyn's request that he come in to find out more about "why I'm the way I am." Evelyn's somatic preoccupations included complaints of pain during intercourse, a long-standing concern since having an abortion several years after the birth of their daughter. As Evelyn's worry about Mark leaving her increased, she actively sought out consultations with various specialists about her pain. After numerous appointments, she found a surgeon who was apparently willing to perform a hysterectomy based on her history of frequent trips to his emergency ward complaining of pain and discomfort. In her therapy sessions Evelyn indicated that she didn't want any more children and that even though the surgeon was not promising the procedure would result in no pain, she was going to proceed with the operation.

In sessions leading up to the operation, Evelyn revealed more of her fantasy that the removal of the pain would also remove her worries about Mark leaving her. She expressed only mild discomfort at the thought of the procedure and its implications, focusing entirely on the potential calm this would bring to her panic about Mark. I felt awful as I listened to the rationale for this operation and recognized that the motivation for such a major step lay not in the medical necessity for the procedure but in the vain hope of calming the patient's raging anxiety and panic. Efforts at helping the patient see this and reconsider met with little success. Finally, within one week of the operation, Evelyn consented to have me contact the surgeon and discuss with him both her emotional concerns and her tendency to overfocus on physical concerns. In consultation with the surgeon and the patient, the operation was postponed. Marital sessions were suggested to the patient to help discuss Evelyn's true motivation for the operation, and with her support a referral to a marital therapist was arranged. The referral was seen as an opportunity to open up more communication between the couple and provide a chance for Evelyn to address her needs in a more honest way.

This scenario illustrates some of the conflicts and issues involved in work with borderline patients. The presence of familial and marital components are often at the heart of the patient's presentations, and sometimes it is both unavoidable and even mandatory that these issues be addressed. It is simply not possible to do this within traditional one-to-one psychotherapy. Some therapists feel comfortable bringing family members into the sessions. Others do not and make referrals to marital or family therapists while retaining the potential for individual work either during or after the conjoint sessions. Regardless of the perspective, this case argues strongly for the involvement of the husband and the need for an immediate response to a highly pressurized situation.

The sections that follow explore each of the options mentioned earlier and review the value of each in expanding the treatment approach with the borderline patient.

As the discussion on consultation indicated, there are times in our work with borderline patients when concern about their functioning will lead us to consider a hospital admission. At these junctures a number of important considerations need to be taken into account before implementing a referral. These issues focus most frequently on the question of regression and the result of introducing into the patient's life another powerful force that will most certainly prompt reactions based on the patient's dependency needs and chronic desires to be taken care of. So let's discuss both inpatient and day hospital settings and the role they can play in the treatment of the borderline patient.

Inpatient Admissions

The need for an inpatient stay is perhaps most obvious when the issue of suicidality is present. Here we are called on to respond to the patient's potential self-harm; the risk accompanying such concern may make it feel as if there is no option but to admit the patient.

Two important areas of consideration may help guide us when faced with a suicidal patient. The first involves the question of whether the crisis represents an acute risk or a more chronic concern. This important information can help the therapist determine more of the risk factor, as acute suicidal impulses tend to be potentially more dangerous than chronic self-harm ideation.

The second area of exploration is really a subset of the first and involves clarifying whether the current crisis represents a true suicidal risk or a reflection of the borderline patient's need to have someone assume a caretaking role. This determination is vitally important, allowing the therapist to avoid if possible an unnecessary hospitalization.

There has been much written about the benefits or detriments of hospitalization for the borderline patient. In brief, the argument may be summarized in the following way: for those of us who view the borderline condition as amenable to change and adaptation through intensive psychotherapeutic involvement, a hospitalization can be a useful extension of a long-term psychotherapeutic treatment plan, with regressions perceived as opportunities to help us understand the patient's inner world.

But for those who believe that the borderline will be best helped by stabilization and the creation of concrete goals, hospitalization will be viewed as negative because of its fostering of regression. The goals of a hospital stay—often undertaken with a preset discharge target date—will then be those of short-term stabilization, providing the patient with a brief respite before the return to community life.

In addition to the use of hospitalization with suicidal patients, an inpatient admission may be therapeutic with profoundly rageful or impulsive patients at times of acute crisis or decompensation. Here the goals of the stay may be similar to those just described for the brief stabilization model. A short stay aimed at helping the patient contain the rage and reconstitute his functioning can be helpful both in preventing more serious dysfunctional behavior and in alerting the patient to the potential for receiving support and structure at times when these feelings are most challenged by troublesome affect.

Once a patient has been hospitalized, two auxiliary aspects of the admission that may also prove useful to the therapeutic process involve the diagnosis of other clinical conditions and the evaluation of the patient's appropriateness for individual psychotherapy. Often affective disorders, panic disorders, and eating disorders can accompany the diagnosis of a Borderline Personality Disorder, and their presence and severity are important considerations in developing treatment goals. Having a patient in the hospital and exposed to a multidisciplinary team provides the opportunity for a thorough diagnostic workup and offers input on the presence of Axis I diagnoses, the role of medication in treatment, and the focus and scope of individual psychotherapy following discharge.

Day Hospital Admissions

Unlike the inpatient hospital unit, most day programs focus on increasing the patient's functioning level as opposed to addressing an acute problem area. As a result, patients with acute suicidal potential or in the midst of psychotic episodes are not referred for day hospital consideration. The day hospital, often built around the model of a therapeutic milieu, relies heavily on group therapy as the primary mode of treatment. Its emphasis on daily or structured attendance, its full-day programming, and its expectation of good attendance and participation mirror the work setting. This is no coincidence, as the underlying principle of the day treatment option is to stress the patient's abilities and emphasize the healthier aspects of the patient's functioning. By virtue of these expectations the day hospital is less tolerant of the patient adopting a sick role and more active in fostering a return to previous levels of functioning outside the program.

This option can be extremely effective for the borderline patient. The expectation of healthier functioning and worklike standards of performance provides a structure of interaction that can be both supportive and containing. The decision not to remove the patient totally from her home or work environment can help lessen the regressive nature of the dependency. Leaving the patient responsible for herself helps to maintain her access to family and friends. It also maintains a sense of normalcy in her life and overtly sends a message that the focus of treatment is a return to successful community involvement.

The day hospital program may also be a bridge to other rehabilitation or training programs. As a step in emphasizing group functioning, working with expectations about performance levels and interpersonal dynamics, the day hospital objectives of returning an individual to higher levels of functioning can provide the borderline patient with the blueprint for a structured and predictable path to work-related activity in the community. The usually high staff-patient ratio offers opportunities to explore feelings with many different therapists across numerous disciplinary and skill areas. The worklike length of the day allows for the scheduling of several different kinds of activities, ranging from group therapy sessions, communication skills and anger management, to relaxation and recreation hours. The mixed nature of the programming addresses many of the social and individual needs that some of our borderline patients have in structuring their leisure time and organizing their daily responsibilities.

Group Therapy

As either an adjunct or an alternative to individual psychotherapy, group therapy has been identified as a mode of treatment that has many benefits for this population. Group work provides the patient with the opportunity to be involved with people in close and intense relations without necessarily having to establish ongoing, emotionally close friendships. The nature of the group experience also provides the patient with the chance both to observe and to participate in a wide range of interaction. Watching how people respond to one another, seeing how anger is dealt with, and observing how people take risks in group settings can help educate the borderline patient about how other people manage their conflicts. Working with others who are seeking assistance about troubling problems can also help in the development of empathy and tolerance, aspects of emotional maturity that sometimes elude the borderline in the crush to get their needs met.

Not all group models are equally effective in providing these opportunities for the borderline patient. Evaluation of group work suggests that borderline patients do better in groups that emphasize the here-and-now functioning of the group dynamic. Borderlines also require an active and guiding group leader who will prevent harmful regressive conflicts and guarantee a safe and secure group environment. The therapy group becomes a safety net for the patient, a holding environment that is both reliable and predictable in its structure and its boundaries.

With the establishment of these parameters, the group experience can offer a mode of treatment that can either complement or replace individual psychotherapy. The emphasis on the here and now focuses attention on the patient's behavior in the group, thus avoiding the difficulties of having to rely on the patient's reports of past events and feelings. The structure of the group can also help minimize transferences and regression and lessen the patient's exclusive dependence on the therapist. The opportunity to offer and receive advice from others provides practice that can contribute to the development of self-esteem, lessen the patient's ability to distort, deny, or avoid, and even include chances for confrontation and reconciliation. For many borderline patients, however, and for the group leaders, the sense is that an ongoing therapeutic contact outside the group is also necessary, providing a place where the borderline patient can examine and evaluate the group interaction.

The three case studies in this chapter have illustrated some of the complex feelings and problematic elements of work with borderline patients. The act of choosing a therapeutic approach and setting for these patients is, as has been indicated, a difficult and challenging process. Those of us who are accustomed to working in individual psychotherapy and helping our patients gain insight into their functioning may find ourselves both frustrated and failing with the borderline patient who needs more all the time yet appears sorely incapable of making gains.

My premise in this chapter has been that if we pay attention to the borderline's neediness and helplessness, then we may realize he does not necessarily need "more of the same," no matter how skillful and committed the current treatment is. These patients require a multitude of ways to connect with others, to harness their runaway dependency needs, and to curb their regressive tendencies. Having a repertoire of numerous settings, techniques, and approaches can allow us to be involved with the patient in a different manner, guiding but perhaps not directing treatment and observing and interacting in more structured and hence less threatening exchanges. Considering how to complement and expand on individual psychotherapy by combining treatment modes for the BPD patient is simply a response to and a recognition of the challenging nature of these patients and the very diverse ways in which their needs must be approached.

NOTES

P. 52, *The question of why therapeutic work:* Levy, J. (1992). The borderline patient: Psychotherapeutic stalemates. In D. Silver & M. Rosenbluth (Eds.), *Handbook of borderline disorders* (pp. 307–334). Madison, CT: International Universities Press.

P. 54, *Just as no one theoretical perspective:* Paris, J. (1994). *Borderline personality disorder: A multidimensional approach.* Washington, DC: American Psychiatric Press.

P. 54, *Understanding borderline patients' needs:* Giovacchini, P. L. (1993). *Borderline patients, the psychosomatic focus, and the therapeutic process.* Northvale, NJ: Jason Aronson.

P. 56, *For many of these patients, the regression:* Adler, G. (1985). *Borderline psychopathology and its treatment.* Northvale, NJ: Jason Aronson.

P. 60, *The regression and its impact:* Shapiro, E. R. (1992). Family dynamics and borderline personality disorder. In D. Silver and M. Rosenbluth (Eds.), *Handbook of borderline disorders* (pp. 471–494). Madison, CT: International Universities Press.

P. 61, *The therapist's feelings:* Gabbard, G. O., & Wilkinson, S. M. (1994). *Management of countertransference with borderline patients.* Washington, DC: America Psychiatric Press.

P. 65, *Acute care can be understood:* Frances, A., Clarkin, J., & Perry, S. (1984). *Differential therapeutics in psychiatry: The art and science of treatment selection.* New York: Brunner/Mazel.

P. 66, *While considering consultation may appear simple:* Levy, J. (1992). The borderline patient: Psychotherapeutic stalemates. In D. Silver and M. Rosenbluth (Eds.), *Handbook of borderline disorders* (pp. 307–334). Madison, CT: International Universities Press.

P. 73, *The need for an inpatient stay:* Rosenbluth, M., & Silver, D. (1992). The inpatient treatment of borderline personality disorder. In D. Silver & M. Rosenbluth (Eds.), *Handbook of borderline disorders* (pp. 509–532). Madison, CT: International Universities Press.

P. 76, *As either an adjunct . . . , group therapy:* Leszcz, M. (1992). Group psychotherapy of the borderline patient. In D. Silver & M. Rosenbluth (Eds.), *Handbook of borderline disorders* (pp. 435–470). Madison, CT: International Universities Press.

PSYCHOTHERAPY OF BORDERLINE PATIENTS

Jerome Kroll

This chapter will present an approach to the treatment of borderline patients based on basic principles of supportive and exploratory psychotherapy. I develop a distinction between focusing in therapy on content or on process, and apply these considerations to the types of problems that borderline patients bring to psychotherapy. Particular attention is paid to the current linkage between childhood sexual abuse and borderline symptoms.

The model presented here is based on my own experience in working with borderline patients. It acknowledges the consequences of childhood abuse but focuses on competent functioning in present life rather than on encouraging excessive memory retrieval and abreactions that propel the patient in a downward regressive spiral.

CHARACTERISTICS OF BORDERLINE PERSONALITY DISORDER

In order to discuss treatment of borderlines intelligently (and intelligibly), we need to discuss first what we mean by borderline. Of all the categories listed in *DSM-III* and *DSM-IV*,

Borderline Personality Disorder (BPD) has perhaps generated the most prolonged and acrimonious disagreements. Ongoing questions of proper descriptors (criteria), etiology, relationship to other disorders of both Axis I and II, and optimal treatment modalities all raise very strong suspicions that there is a lack of clarity about the very concept of Borderline Personality Disorder.

If we may ignore issues of etiology for the moment, we can say that the term *Borderline Personality Disorder* refers to an enduring pattern of behaviors, dispositions, and temperament characterized by the following:

- Impulsivity and emotional instability
- A dramatic interpersonal style that tends to shift between idealization and devaluation
- Cognitive difficulties that manifest under stress as mild disorganization (confusion) and transient altered states of consciousness
- An inclination to think of oneself as a victim and to gravitate toward situations that either directly or symbolically reinforce the victim status

When we read the voluminous literature on BPD, it becomes clear that researchers and clinicians tend to discover in their patients those borderline symptoms that best conform to their own theoretical notions of BPD in the first place. If the therapist has a bias to conceptualize borderline in terms of its relationship to the affective disorders, greater attention will be paid to the patient's emotional instability and impulsivity. If the therapist's bias is toward a posttraumatic stress syndrome secondary to childhood sexual and physical abuse, then emphasis will be on self-injurious and other victimization behaviors as well as on dissociative experiences. It is obvious that this degree of polarization in the basic conceptualization of borderline will be reflected in a similar polarization of treatment approaches.

Historically, the very notion of Borderline Personality Disorder originated in the observation that certain patients who seemed to have several characteristics in common were uncommonly difficult to treat in psychotherapy. It has also been observed that the treatment of what are now designated as Axis I disorders, such as depressive and anxiety conditions, is enormously complicated and much less successful when borderline traits are prominent. Thus it is not surprising that "difficult to treat" remains the enduring characteristic of Borderline Personality Disorder and sets the stage for the zealousness with which clinicians representing different therapeutic techniques advocate their own approach and condemn others.

BASIC PRINCIPLES

It is my strong contention that the difficulties that therapists encounter when treating borderlines stem primarily from the neglect of basic principles that apply to all sound psychotherapy. Paradoxically, the arduousness of treating borderlines and the trepidation with which many therapists engage in therapy of such patients lead the therapists to think that borderlines, being so special, require a special type of therapy in which the usual therapeutic principles are ineffective and therefore do not apply. Such an attitude can result in a variety of unproductive and, at times, disastrous approaches to therapy, two of which will be outlined here.

The first, which can more accurately be called the lack of an approach, consists of a hodgepodge of protective attitudes (such as telling the patient that she is not ready to look for work), pop psychology clichés (responding with "well, at least you tried" to all of the patient's failures rather than examining how the patient may engage in self-sabotage), and suggestions designed to prevent the presumably fragile patient from feeling so badly about herself (helping the patient place the blame on others). This relatively naive approach leaves the bewildered therapist usually two steps behind, desperately trying to figure out how to respond to the latest in a series of crises created by the patient's self-destructive and acting-out behaviors.

The second and opposite therapeutic approach, rigidly structured rather than chaotic, derives from a strong adherence to a specialized theory-driven method that shapes and interprets much of the patient's past and present experiences in terms of a favored hypothesis about borderlines. The hypothesis in vogue now is that all problems that the borderline has can be traced to experiences of childhood sexual abuse, and all treatment endeavors should be directed at recovery of memories of this abuse.

In criticizing these opposite approaches to the treatment of borderlines, I make two basic assumptions: first, that there are core principles that apply to all psychotherapy and, second, that these principles are foundational to any specialized approaches to therapy with borderlines. This means that specialized approaches must build on, rather than ignore or replace, basic therapeutic principles. Finally, I make the further assumptions that because of the very nature of borderline reactivity and vulnerability, it is critically important to pay more rather than less attention to basic therapeutic principles, and that disregarding the fundamentals of what constitutes good psychotherapy will land the therapist and patient in deeper difficulty, and with greater rapidity, than that which ordinarily occurs when working with other types of patients.

Modalities of Therapy

One of the cardinal principles of psychotherapy is the distinction made between supportive and exploratory modes of therapy and between content and process methods of conducting therapy. Figure 4.1 displays in graphic form the four combinations that can be derived from this two-by-two configuration.

Realistically, pure forms of therapy in which all the interactions occur exclusively in just one of the four boxes do not exist.

	Supportive	Exploratory
C **o** **n** **t** **e** **n** **t**	*Window A* Openly supportive Behavioral-didactic focus Problem solving Competency based	*Window B* Explores patterns in life events

P
r
o
c
e
s
s
	Window C
	
	Identifies process
	  occurring in therapy
	Provides support for
	  changing the process with
	  the goal of increasing
	  competency
		Window D
		
		Explores process
		  occurring in therapy
		Explores relationship
		  of therapy process
		  to life patterns

Figure 4.1
Modalities of Therapy

Most therapies are combinations of these components, varying across time, stage of therapy, and external circumstances. The two treatment modalities that probably come closest to a pure form are psychoanalytic and cognitive-behavioral therapies, and neither is the focus of this chapter.

Supportive-type interactions range from specific problem-solving discussions to positive assessments of the patient's virtues and abilities designed to offset a negative self-image and encourage giving up old ways and attempting new ones. Exploratory-type interactions encompass routine history taking and eventually the utilization of such information to perceive, label, and discuss maladaptive patterns of behaviors. The assumption here is that awareness of maladaptive patterns is a necessary although not sufficient basis to changing such behaviors. The therapeutic risk in pointing out patterns is that the patient hears these comments merely as criticism, not as something to be examined and used as a starting point for change. Exploratory modes also involve examination of transference behaviors in the microcosm of therapy, allowing assumptions and responses about the outside world to be scrutinized firsthand in the therapy session.

The content-process model complements the supportive-exploratory model. Content refers to the topic that the patient and therapist are discussing; process refers to the style of interaction in which they are discussing a topic. The content can be an exploration of the patient's history, practical problem-solving techniques, or an examination of the process that is occurring in therapy. There is always a process going on in therapy; the critical issue is whether the process occurs without examination or whether the process itself is automatically monitored and commented on when appropriate.

For example, it is helpful for a therapist to recognize that the therapy is operating in a supportive mode in order to think about whether this is what she means to do. It is a therapeutic choice whether to identify this process (supportive mode) openly to the patient or just to continue to be supportive. Such reflection can help the therapist recognize when she has crossed a boundary between reasonable support and intrusive or excessive caretaking. There are benefits and risks to each choice, and given the complexity of human beings, we can create no absolute guidelines. The therapist has to weigh many factors, but fundamental to conducting sound therapy is the self-reflective appreciation of the implications of operating in the different windows depicted in Figure 4.1.

Errors and disasters in therapy frequently reflect what I shall term an injudicious emphasis on a single component rather than a proper balance of supportive and exploratory work and content and process focus. It has been my own experience, both in terms of supervision and practice, that therapists, in their work with borderlines, have tended to lean too heavily on supportive-type interactions while failing to examine the process through which support is given. This has the benefit of reducing, at least temporarily, the anxiety of both the patient and the therapist but carries the risk of infantilizing the patient as well as encouraging the patient to work the therapy so as to continue to have the therapist play an exclusively nurturing role, with little emphasis on working toward change.

Supportive-Exploratory Versus Content-Process Perspectives

The following case provides examples of several types of behaviors commonly seen in therapy with borderline patients, including the use of veiled threats of suicide to propel other people into action, setting up potential conflicts between different therapists, misinterpretation of communication, and, in this particular situation, drug-seeking behaviors.

A . B .

Mr. A.B. is a thirty-four-year-old divorced man, currently unemployed because of knee pain that seems out of proportion to the physical findings. He has a history of substance abuse, of self-injurious behaviors that required hospitalization in his twenties, and of demanding and unsuccessful relationships with significant others. One weekend day, I received a call from A.B.'s pain clinic doctor who related that he suggested and A.B. agreed to a brief psychiatric hospitalization since he would not give A.B. any more pain medications, and there was an inference that he might be suicidal. I arranged hospitalization, but A.B. never arrived. He called me three days later, wanting to know why I thought he would benefit from hospitalization. Rather than entering into a discussion in which I persuaded him how hospitalization could help him, I told him that I thought it was he who had wanted to come into the hospital and that I was merely assisting him. I then voiced surprise that he would ask me to list the benefits, other than suicide prevention, of hospitalization, when he knew that it was up to him to make such a determination. He ended the conversation by asking me to prescribe some pain medications, which I politely declined.

If we look at this brief interaction in terms of the categories that were presented earlier, it seems clear that A.B. opened the contact with a "content" question—namely, why did I think he would benefit from hospitalization. I could have given him a "content" reply: that he needed to learn other skills for pain relief, that he was in crisis during that weekend, that I wanted to make sure he was in a safe place. Such answers, whether accurate or not, would have remained on the same content plane as his question and would have avoided examining his behavior with me.

On the one hand, had I chosen to explain why I thought hospitalization might be indicated, he most likely would have argued with me that it would not be helpful. The content might have been whether or not there were benefits in hospitalization, but the process would have been a nonproductive argument (at many levels) between patient and therapist.

In this example, I tried to avoid the quagmire of content. On the other hand, I did not go quite so far as to confront him with a "process" response—that he had set up a sequence of events in which his pain doctor offered him a hospital bed and now he was wanting to know why I thought he should be in the hospital. Essentially, I hovered somewhere in the process-exploratory realm.

When A.B. shifted the conversation to a request for pain medications, I decided not to process this with him, such as wondering if the point of the call in the first place was an attempt to get medications. I answered on a simple content level without processing the request; the answer was that I would not prescribe pain medications for him. I chose not to comment on the obvious, which is that he knew I would not because we had discussed this issue before. This type of comment could only be taken as a smug criticism of him and could not be helpful at such a time.

This is an extended discussion for such a brief interaction, but the essential point remains clear. All interactions take place on both the supportive-exploratory continuum and the process-content continuum. It is the therapist's task to select, within the few seconds that are available for decision making in the give-and-take of a conversation, the type of answer and interaction that appears to be the most suitable therapeutic response at that moment, keeping in mind the long-term view.

BORDERLINES AND CHILDHOOD SEXUAL ABUSE

Since treatment of borderline patients in the 1990s so often seems to involve some degree of incest and childhood trauma work, I will next discuss a case that includes these components in order to look further at supportive-exploratory and content-process interventions.

C . D .

C.D. is a thirty-one-year-old divorced woman, living with a boyfriend and working full time as a home health aide. She has a history of more than ten hospitalizations for self-injurious behaviors and suicide threats but has shown increasing stability in the past two years. She is now in her first relationship with a male who has not been overtly abusive to her. In a therapy session, she noted that her boyfriend became upset with her because she spaced out while they were in a restaurant. He complained that C.D. always did this and ruined their evenings. I asked C.D. what she thought happened to her at such times and why she thought it might be happening. C.D. had no idea. She recognized that it happened to her but could not identify the antecedents nor was she aware that it was anything she was doing on purpose. She was aware, however, that this vague, detached state was somehow pleasant to her.

I inquired about the situation in the restaurant. C.D. then recalled that some young girls dressed in ballet costumes were sitting with their mother in the adjacent booth at the restaurant. This seemingly innocent scenario had stirred some uneasiness in her and perhaps even a vague memory trace about her own childhood experiences of sexual abuse and about the vulnerability in general of young girls to such abuse. With this train of thought, she had almost automatically begun to space out in the restaurant. I asked what types of memories had been stirred up, at which point C.D. began to drift off right there in the office.

I immediately interrupted the process to call C.D.'s attention to what had just happened, told her that I did not need or want to know what memories had begun to arise, and requested that she identify what had just happened to her as an experience of drifting off and not to let it happen. C.D. was able to do this, at which point she and I were able to recognize her general tendency to deal with many sorts of stressful situations, cognitions, and feeling states by drifting off. I suggested that C.D. think about practicing not letting herself tune out, which required, of course, paying attention to stimuli that triggered such reactions and becoming aware of her own expert ability to tune out rapidly.

In this case, the session began in the content mode, with the patient's description of a brief but multilayered event in a restaurant. I asked the patient to think about triggering mechanisms that bring about a transient altered state of consciousness ("drifting off"). A further content-exploratory inquiry (about the memories) actually produced right in the office the beginnings of a drifting off episode. At this point, I interrupted the process, which had focused on the content of what had happened in the restaurant, in order to point out to the patient the change in the therapy interaction that had just occurred.

In essence, the patient was beginning to dissociate, and the therapist interrupted this, asking her consciously and deliberately to recognize the dissociation and to bring herself back to the present. The focus was no longer on external content (the events in the restaurant) and manifestly shifted away from memory retrieval of childhood sexual abuse events; instead, the focus became an examination of the process that had just happened in the therapy session itself. After this was accomplished, the therapy session shifted again to a supportive mode in which the patient was asked to develop better skills at recognizing the beginnings of a dissociative state and at interrupting such shifts of consciousness in order to stay in the present.

The Dangers of Regressive Therapy

The discussion of why I chose to switch from content to process and back again and from exploratory to supportive modes brings us to some general considerations of therapy with borderlines who report histories of childhood sexual abuse. I will make some remarks based on this specific case and then backtrack to discuss more theoretical concerns.

The session began fairly routinely, with the patient reporting an event (the restaurant scene) that itself represented a class of occurrences that had given her difficulty recently. However, the very process of narrating the scenario of seeing the young girls in their ballet costumes began to make her uncomfortable right in the therapy session, and then the focused question of what memories were stirred up began to precipitate a dissociative episode.

My understanding of the standard therapy nowadays regarding childhood sexual abuse is that the goal is to push for more memories, to encourage the patient via imagery and visualization to realize more fully the horror of the events and their consequences in later life. Many therapists believe that the therapeutic process cannot occur without rich details and emotional abreactions to the childhood abuse. I think that this is totally misguided, that it leads to regressive therapy and, what is worse, to regressive behaviors and interactions in the patient's life.

The first problem with regressive therapy is that the details of the abuse do not need to be exposed in order for the patient to improve, especially in the case of borderline patients who dissociate and engage in self-injurious behaviors when remembering childhood trauma. There is nothing helpful or adaptive in having a patient spend half or more of a therapy session in an altered state of consciousness. The patient already spends too much time in such states when not in therapy. The patient needs to be present in therapy for therapeutic work to get done. Endless indulgence in old miseries perpetuates a victim mentality and does nothing to help the patient change old maladaptive patterns.

In the case of C.D., I recognized the incipient appearance of a dissociated state, called the patient's attention to it, and used the therapy as a microcosm for understanding and changing a fairly prevalent style of C.D.'s personal and social interaction. The details of the abuse do not matter now, for several reasons. First of all, we know that childhood memories are distorted, may merge several different events with an admixture of fantasized and later embellished images, and are susceptible to influence by suggestions of the therapist. But even if we assume that this particular memory was fairly accurate, the patient had demonstrated that she was not able to retrieve and hold the memory images and the accompanying emotions and self-critical judgments without going into a self-induced trance. If the details of the memory are important—and they may well be in terms of specific symptoms that are driven by the details of abuse—they will still have to be placed on hold until the patient is able, if ever, to work on traumatic memories without becoming dysfunctional and self-destructive.

The second problem with an exclusively abuse-focused therapy is that abuse usually occurs in the larger context of dysfunctional households, in which neglect, emotional coldness, reversed parent-child roles (other than sexual) and other poor role-modeling experiences, alcohol and substance abuse, and the child's own method of finding meaning (or nonmeaning) in such an environment are all important factors that contribute to the development of this particular person.

Third, abuse-focused therapy runs the risk of encouraging either a sense of victimization or of unqualified outrage that is not conducive to progress in life.

With these considerations in mind, I switched from content to process when the examination of content threatened to overwhelm the patient; I labeled for the patient what was happening (she was beginning to dissociate) and suggested, by way of supportive comments, that she in fact could exercise some control over alterations in her levels of consciousness. I specifically offered the viewpoint that retrieval of memories at this time was ill advised because staying in the present was much more important. Finally, I suggested that C.D. identify to her boyfriend what is happening when it is happening so that he will understand what has occurred rather than taking it as a personal comment on how C.D. feels about him.

Since borderline patients often have trouble framing simple and straightforward communications, I even offered an example of the type of words that she could use to explain this to her boyfriend: "I began to space out because the children in ballet costumes stirred up some painful memories for me." Phrasing it this way keeps it clear that the boyfriend is not being asked to become a therapist to C.D. or to become adept in bringing her out of dissociative states. That is C.D.'s task. If C.D. and her boyfriend can go out for a casual dinner and enjoy themselves and use this pleasant occasion as one more piece of positive interaction on which a solid relationship can be built, and if such occasions can be multiplied by avoiding "spacing out," then the therapy session will have been more helpful than the endless pursuit of painful memories would have been.

TREATMENT GOALS

In working with borderline patients, it is important to have treatment objectives. What are the short- and long-term goals? What major problems can we anticipate will develop in the therapy of borderline patients, particularly (although not exclusively) those with histories of childhood sexual abuse? The goals and the problems are in one sense generic and in another sense specific to what we mean by borderline.

Essentially, the goals of therapy are to increase the patient's competency in functioning in the world. This includes competency in relevant areas of interpersonal relationships, marriage, work, parenthood, creativity, and spirituality. It also includes competency in one's sense of self as a reasonably integrated, responsible, and autonomous person who lives within a community. These goals are ethnocentrically derived—that is, they embody the value system of Western culture and may not fully express value systems of other cultures—but they can also be seen as fairly universal for human society. I need to clarify that the goals of therapy are not to strive for perfection but are merely to work toward as much competency as the person can manage. There is a tendency to mistake specialized techniques for actual goals. Thus, expressing anger, elaborating more and more memories, and abreacting past traumas are not goals in themselves; functioning more competently is the goal.

Problems that arise in working with borderlines are similar to those seen in all psychotherapy, but they take on a certain urgency and dramatic quality because of how borderlines act out and how transference difficulties emerge in their therapy. Both in and out of therapy, borderline patients appear driven by predominant themes of reworking early issues of dependency and victimization. These assume particular salience when there is a background of childhood abuse, but they appear to be common and often intertwined themes with most borderline individuals.

Dealing with Dependency

The following case illustrates the ways in which intertwined problems of dependency and victimization show up both in real life—in the form of maintaining an unhealthy relationship—and in therapy—in the form of "getting" the therapist, a male psychology intern, to tell the patient what to do.

E . F .

Ms. E.F. is a twenty-eight-year-old graduate student who started therapy because she wished to extricate herself from what she perceived was yet another unhealthy relationship with a man. She had marked identity problems and chronic feelings of emptiness. She had previously been in therapy and on medication for depressions that appeared precipitated by stormy breakups with boyfriends. Her present boyfriend, working in a local insurance office, had become very possessive of her, following her around town, telephoning at all hours, and being generally unpleasant. He had on occasion threatened to kill her, himself, or both. Much time was spent in therapy developing safety plans, examining legal options, and looking at different ways of disengaging from the boyfriend.

E.F. finally decided to move to an apartment in the suburbs, hoping to attain some degree of distance and anonymity. She proceeded with her plans to have a small moving company help her, but the day before the scheduled move, she called her boyfriend, told him her plans, and asked him to help her with the move. E.F. was embarrassed at having to tell this to her therapist at the next session, convinced that he would be angry with her.

The therapist belatedly recognized that he needed to shift from content to process and, during the next six months, helped E.F. to connect her predominant feeling of emptiness with her identity disturbance, which consisted of defining herself as a victim. The focus for this work began with an exploration of why E.F. was certain that the therapist would be angry with her and what he had done to contribute to this expectation. This enabled E.F. to become less dependent on her boyfriend, who slowly disengaged as he found a more psychologically obliging girlfriend.

This case captures typical borderline themes of dependency and victimization. E.F. and her therapist were caught up in the content of how to ensure E.F.'s safety and failed to consider the extent of her attachment to the boyfriend, her dependency on his presence in her life, and the role that her fantasies about being the victim of his passion and aggression played in her behaviors in maintaining the relationship.

I need to state here briefly that I am not blaming E.F. or suggesting that anything she did justified or excused the boyfriend's intimidations. The responsibility for male predatory behavior lies with the man. But it was E.F., not the boyfriend, who was in therapy, and the therapist was called on to do more than support E.F. in developing safety plans. In this particular case, the focus had to shift from supportive to exploratory work in order to help provide E.F. with some labels (victimization behaviors) and schemata for understanding and changing an old pattern of presenting herself as helpless—a presentation to which both the boyfriend and the therapist had responded.

The next case illustrates another aspect of the therapeutic problem of how to respond to the borderline patient's signals of distress in a manner that is helpful but that does not reinforce victimization or dependency patterns.

G . H .

Ms. G.H. is a thirty-two-year-old office worker with a history of sexual abuse throughout childhood by her grandfather. Her adult relationships with men have been marked by a series of disappointing love affairs. In one therapy session, she spoke about her essential feeling of unattractiveness, thinking that if she were a good enough person and a beautiful enough woman, boyfriends would not leave her.

At the next therapy session, the therapist, a middle-aged male social worker, sensed her emotional pain and complimented her on her appearance. G.H. was initially flattered but then began to wonder about the comment, specifically whether it indicated that the therapist was sexually interested in her. She did not think so but could not help developing some romantic thoughts about him.

She paid particular attention to her dress and grooming for the next session, but the therapist made no comment about her appearance. G.H. was very upset but did not speak to this issue. She tried to figure out whether the therapist was now being coy or truly did not care at all about her. She ruminated about this all evening and finally interrupted this mood state by bingeing and vomiting a few times. Several sessions later, she told the therapist what had happened. His assurances that she must have misunderstood his compliment because he did not have sexual feelings for her were not particularly helpful.

This type of situation is not uncommon in therapy with borderline patients. The therapist, based on his own issues and vulnerabilities, was distressed at the patient's distress and tried to remedy it by remarks meant to negate the patient's negative self-images. Sometimes, this is a very legitimate thing to do. There is a place in therapy for validating a patient's worth and challenging self-critical attitudes, for indicating that one cares, for encouraging remarks, and for nurturing. But too often such attempts by the therapist also feed into a borderline patient's vulnerability to what is perceived as sexual flattery or as intentions to increase her dependency on the therapist.

It might make sense to tell a patient who believes that she is stupid that she is really quite bright, but it is naive for a male therapist to tell a patient who thinks she is ugly that she is really very attractive. While challenging a patient's negative self-perceptions may be an important piece of the therapeutic work, proper attention must be paid to the patient's life history of positive and negative interactions with others and to the possible meaning of the comments in light of transference and countertransference issues.

BORDERLINES WITH PTSD

Although the weight of scientific evidence argues that childhood sexual and physical abuse are general risk factors for the development of many types of psychiatric problems in adolescence and adulthood, there does appear to be a particularly close correlation between certain types of borderline symptoms, such as dissociative episodes and self-injurious behaviors, and the more severe experiences of childhood abuse. It has been helpful in many instances to view such borderline patients as suffering from a chronic form of Posttraumatic Stress Disorder, in which a variety of dissociative and self-injurious behaviors represent the chronic responses to having been raised in a highly noxious and stressful environment. The cardinal groupings of PTSD symptoms (intrusive reexperiencing of the traumatic events; persistent avoidance of stimuli reminiscent of the events, along with psychic numbing; persistent symptoms of increased psychological and physiological arousal) are seen prominently in many borderline patients with abuse histories.

I need to point out here that there is much controversy related to the strength of the causal relationship between abuse and borderline problems, and even more controversy about which therapeutic techniques should be used to treat such patients. As suggested earlier, my position regarding this controversy is that there is heuristic value to viewing much borderline psychopathology as stemming from childhood abusive experiences, while still maintaining an appreciation of all the problems involved in distortion of memory retrieval and in irresponsible therapy by overly zealous therapists.

In working with patients with borderline symptoms who have histories of childhood sexual abuse, can we find a way to proceed in therapy without bringing about major dysfunctional regressions into self-injurious behaviors, more and more frequent dissociative episodes, and the creative emergence of improbable memories of, say, satanic cult abuse? The old adage of "no pain, no gain" is extremely naive as a justification for having a patient decompensate under pressure from a therapist to bring up ever deeper and deeper and earlier and earlier memories of abuse.

Essentially, I feel the paradoxical stance is warranted that in therapy memory work, whatever this may specifically mean, cannot be done until the patient is competent to handle such work without resort to self-injurious behaviors or a major breakdown in many of life's important functions. As an alternative, the therapist can adopt a framework of three broad categories to explore in relation to toxic childhood experiences:

1. Coming to terms with the abuse of the past
2. Looking at how the past controls the present
3. Examining how the past controls the transference

There is nothing magical or all-inclusive about these three categories, nor are they necessarily worked on in this particular sequence in therapy. These categories are just a way of organizing an approach to therapy that takes into account the importance of childhood traumas and tries to make some sense of the frequently chaotic presentation of symptoms and crises that borderline patients bring to the work. Most important, such a framework shifts focus away from getting lost in painful memory retrieval and places it on the consequences of the abuse with an eye toward positive change.

Coming to Terms with the Abuse of the Past

It is a truism that the past cannot be changed. Therefore the component of therapy that deals with coming to terms with the past consists primarily of a cognitive structuring effort aimed at changing how the patient has come to perceive herself because of past life experiences.

An initial step, however, involves ascertaining and labeling the extent to which the patient is actually having PTSD symptoms—that is, is experiencing intrusive imagery and its physiological accompaniments. Since attempts to avoid these images and their emotional resonances underlie much of borderline pathology—such as self-injurious behaviors, drug abuse, and intolerance for being alone—it is helpful for the patient to begin to identify what sets off his dysfunctional behaviors. The case of C.D. in the restaurant illustrates this point. Although much has been made of the abuse victim's amnesia for the majority of the childhood abuse, the problem in fact is usually an inability to forget, a frequent flooding of the stream of consciousness with imagery and internal dialogues that rapidly become intolerable. A double process of desensitization and practice in turning off distressing imagery before it develops into a dissociative state can be effective in these situations.

In addition to identifying and working with the patient's actual PTSD symptoms, coming to terms with the abuses of the past also involves dealing with the patient's conflict regarding whatever degree of complicity and participation that she feels occurred voluntarily on her part. This is an extremely shameful and painful issue for the patient to examine and carries considerable risk of exacerbating self-blame and increasing self-injurious behaviors. Nevertheless, there are times when this issue is so intrusive in the patient's life that it must be dealt with, albeit extremely cautiously.

Looking at How the Past Controls the Present

In essence, much of therapy consists of an exploration and solution, however partial, of the ongoing impact of the abusive past on the patient's present life. Themes that are prominent in this regard include the generalization of dissociative episodes as a response to an increasing variety of stressful and emotionally arousing situations that are not linked directly to abuse experiences; self-hatred as a complex response to what the patient has suffered; self-identification as a victim who is fated to live out and, at times, seek out new experiences in which the patient will once again be the victim; a deficient sense of self as having no reality other than as a victim or as a target of other people's exploitation; mistrust of others; and, what is particularly disturbing to the patient, aggressiveness as a result of identification in many ways with the aggressor.

It is clear that there is considerable overlap across these various categories. The themes are mentioned separately here so that we may identify them, but in actuality, self-hatred and a deficient sense of self, for example, are different ways of experiencing and describing the same emotions and cognitions.

The following case illustrates the intrusion into a borderline patient's day-to-day life of a style of relating to those she loves that she is clearly distressed about, since it represents an identification with aggressive components of her childhood environment.

I . J .

Ms. I.J. is a forty-two-year-old legal assistant, living in a relatively stable lesbian relationship with a partner for the past seven years. The stormy borderline behaviors and interpersonal conflicts seen in her twenties and early thirties have, for the most part, subsided. Her present relationship has become problematic recently because of I.J.'s increased teasing of her partner, which has passed the limits of playfulness and has become verbally cruel and hurtful. While teasing has been a long-standing trait of I.J., its escalation in terms of intensity and maliciousness even surprises I.J. herself at times. After considerable examination in therapy, I.J. has been able to connect this to her father's renewed attempts to establish contact with I.J. in a way that recreated the childhood pattern of father and daughter forming a conspiracy of sarcasm against an ineffective mother. I.J., as a child, could win her father's approval by acting like him, although this never prevented for more than a few moments his turning against her with physical and sexual aggression.

The work in therapy consisted, in part, of I.J. appreciating the different ways in which she had incorporated aspects of her cruel father into her own style of interacting, especially toward those who were important to her. If the same sarcasm were to begin to show up in the therapy situation, as it often does, then it would need to be dealt with as an instance of transference. This gives the therapist an opportunity to experience directly, although in a much diluted form, how the patient in childhood had experienced her aggressor.

Discussion in therapy of a patient's identification with the aggressor is often a very painful process, since it requires recognizing traits in herself that she ordinarily dislikes. It means that the adult has now become similar to the person she vowed she would never resemble. Of course, this happens to most of us with regard to at least a few traits that we dislike in our parents, but the universality of this discovery in each of us does not diminish its special relevance in borderline adults who have been abused as children.

Examining How the Past Influences Transference and Countertransference

The therapist must understand that the borderline patient will play out her transference issues in various disguises and that often these behaviors will dovetail neatly with the therapist's own countertransference issues. Transference behaviors are obviously not unique to borderline patients, but there are several themes that emerge in therapy with borderlines that derive their strength from the particular nature of the damaging life experiences of these patients. Borderline patients have, in general, developed personality styles characterized by intense and close interpersonal engagement, leading inevitably to acting out in the transference the distorted personal relationships experienced in childhood. Prominent transference themes include sexualization of the therapeutic relationship, as well as testing the therapist for caretaking or rejection. To the extent that the therapist responds to these transference overtures and behaviors, the patient's destructive and denigrating beliefs about himself and the world are confirmed.

The borderline patient's transference themes have their counterparts in the therapist's personal vulnerabilities: rejection of the patient when therapy becomes arduous or when the patient acts out; rationalization by the therapist that a sexual relationship will be therapeutic for the patient; use of the patient as an object of exploitation; effort expended on excessive caretaking activities to assuage the therapist's anxiety about otherwise being an ineffective therapist (and person).

Acting out with the patient can occur in all therapies, but it seems to occur more frequently and more intensely in working with borderlines for all the reasons that make borderlines borderlines. As an example, let us consider the following case.

K . L .

K.L. is a twenty-nine-year-old married woman with two young children. She works part time as a speech therapist. Her marriage has deteriorated into a battle of spite, with each partner trying to upset the other or to demonstrate that the other is not meeting his or her needs.

After several days of threatening to overdose with pills, K.L. was hospitalized in the psychiatric unit of a community hospital. Her husband became contrite, and a temporary truce ensued. K.L. went home on an overnight pass, but the couple began to argue about whether the children should watch one or two hours of television. The husband was cold to K.L. but then wanted to be sexual with her at bedtime. She refused to let him near her; he retreated to the couch where he spent the night.

On returning to the psychiatric unit the next day, K.L. smuggled in several pain pills hidden in a secret pocket of her purse. The nurses asked her about contraband items and did a brief search, but did not find the pills. The following day, K.L. took ten pills (not a dangerous amount) fifteen minutes before her therapy appointment. She then told the therapist what she had done and accused the therapist of not caring enough about her to keep her safe. The therapist became upset with the nursing staff and filed an incident report about this nursing oversight.

As usual, an episode such as this has multiple levels of meaning. There is certainly sufficient material here for a prolonged scrutiny of the manner in which K.L. pursued the battle with her husband by declaring herself the designated patient. In one move, K.L. split the staff, obtained revenge on her husband for his coldness, and placed her own well-being in minor jeopardy. But for purposes of examining the transference and countertransference aspects of this case, we will concentrate on K.L.'s attack on the therapist and his remarkable response.

K.L.'s lament was hardly unusual: you do not care about me, and no one (including my husband) cares enough about me to keep me safe. The therapist, alarmed at such an accusation because he fully considers himself a caring and compassionate individual, protected this image of himself by agreeing with K.L.'s premise that failure to discover the hidden pills was evidence of lack of caring. In a similar way, he had previously aligned himself with K.L. by supporting her image of herself as victim of her husband, thereby also reinforcing her tendency to ignore her own contributions to interpersonal conflict. Suddenly, the therapist too is accused of victimizing K.L. by not caring enough.

It becomes clear how both excessive caring and rejection of the patient can become two sides of an untherapeutic response to a patient's transference behaviors. Even before any discussion of manipulativeness, of triangulating husband and therapist or therapist and staff, or of the use of self-injurious behaviors to perpetuate a victimization role, the therapist needs to point out that he has now been classified in that expanding category of people who do not care.

But there need not have been any question of blame, either of himself or the nursing staff, or of K.L. The game of finding someone to blame only perpetuates old pathological patterns. Acting out within the context of the therapy session, even though it almost always has additional ramifications, requires shifting from content to process, from supportive to exploratory modes. This is the basic principle of psychotherapy with all patients, not just borderlines.

There is not one set of psychotherapeutic principles for working with borderline patients and another set for working with all other patients. The same basic principles of psychotherapy apply to all patients; if anything, one could say that the basic principles apply all the more to borderlines because of the need to pay special attention to the small details of therapeutic interactions with these patients.

The temptation, seemingly irresistible at times, to develop special therapeutic maneuvers for the "special" borderline problems too often ignores basic principles such as respecting a patient's psychological defenses, maintaining proper boundaries, and avoiding overlooking clinical information just because it is contrary to one's chosen borderline theory.

Traditional psychotherapy rests on a recognition of the interrelated but different processes of supportive and exploratory modes and of the reciprocal relationship between focusing on content and focusing on process in psychotherapy. For the majority of work done with the majority of borderlines, the slow, steady pace of therapy should involve the ongoing examination of the here and now, of the patient's present level of functioning. The past is relevant to the extent that it interferes with competent functioning in the present. In order to maintain this focus, the therapist uses an exploratory mode of examining present relationships and reactions within the context of a supportive therapeutic relationship.

FOR FURTHER READING

Frankel, F. H. (1995). Discovering new memories in psychotherapy: Childhood revisited, fantasy, or both? *New England Journal of Medicine, 333* (9), 591–594.

Haaken, J., & Schlaps, A. (1991). Incest resolution therapy and the objectification of sexual abuse. *Psychotherapy, 28* (1), 39–54.

Herman, J. (1992). *Trauma and recovery.* New York: Basic Books.

Kroll, J. L. (1988). *The challenge of the borderline patient.* New York: Norton.

Kroll, J. L. (1993). *PTSD: Borderlines in therapy.* New York: Norton.

Merskey, H. (1995). Multiple personality disorder and false memory syndrome. *British Journal of Psychiatry, 166* (3), 281–283.

Paris, J. (1996). A critical review of recovered memories in psychotherapy. *Canadian Journal of Psychiatry, 41* (4), 201–210.

CHAPTER

5

TREATING THE NARCISSISTIC PERSONALITY DISORDER

Gary Rodin and Sam Izenberg

Ever since Narcissus fell in love with his own reflection, the term *narcissism* has denoted a quality of "self-love" to the exclusion of caring about others. It has since become a common and often pejoratively used term in our culture. More recently, the adjective *narcissistic* has been applied to behaviors or personality characteristics associated with exhibitionism, grandiosity, or self-centeredness. Unfortunately, although these behaviors are usually intended to elicit an admiring response from others, they often evoke negative reactions, in part, because their meaning is misunderstood.

We are both psychiatrists and psychoanalysts who have had an interest in dynamic therapy and in developmental issues applied to a wide range of conditions. We have become disenchanted with theory-driven treatments and prefer approaches and models that are derived from and validated by the subjective experience of patients. In this regard, we have found self psychology to be a useful treatment model, particularly for patients who suffer from disorders of self-experience. Narcissistic personality disorders are of interest to us because we regard them fundamentally as disorders of the self. We have also become interested, through our work at the Toronto Hospital, in secondary disturbances in the sense of self in patients with psychosomatic and medical conditions.

Patients with narcissistic disorders overtly demonstrate grandiosity and inflated self-regard. Underlying these overt characteristics of narcissism, however, is insecurity and self-doubt. What is the self? We use this term here to refer to the typical and relatively consistent ways in which individuals experience themselves and the circumstances and relationships in which they are involved. The most familiar aspect of the self is self-esteem—that is, the positive or negative valuation that individuals assign to themselves. But other aspects of self-experience include a sense of vitality, wholeness, and identity. Disturbances in the sense of self may be evident in feelings of fragmentation or in confusion and uncertainty regarding the sense of identity. Sexual activity or drugs may be pursued by individuals with disorders of the self in order for them to experience a sense of wholeness or vitality. Such individuals may also be troubled with chronic dysphoria, suicidality, hypochondriasis, or vague feelings of aimlessness and emptiness.

Although narcissistic vulnerabilities are common, we are unhappy with the diagnostic label of Narcissistic Personality Disorder (NPD). First, this label may be offensive because of the pejorative connotation of the term *narcissistic* in our culture. For this reason, this label is almost never communicated to the patients to whom it is applied. In some cases, the use of this label reflects a negative attitude of the consultant or therapist toward a patient who is regarded as self-centered, demanding, or irritating. Also, there may be a gender bias in the use of this label. The designation of NPD is often applied pejoratively to men, just as the label of hysterical or Histrionic Personality Disorder is most often applied to women. It is unlikely that these differences are fully explained by the actual prevalence of these disorders in men and women. Finally, the designation of NPD is limited because it is based on external behavior rather than on the underlying psychological problems. In any case, these problems in self-esteem exist on a continuum in the general population. Indeed, none of us is free of these difficulties, which, presumably, are inherent in the human condition.

CLINICAL ISSUES

The term *narcissistic* has been used in many different ways. It is used here to describe activities, behavior, or experiences that serve to maintain or bolster the sense of self. A narcissistic disorder is one in which the regulation of self-experience is impaired and in which many activities or behaviors are required to maintain the sense of self.

The diagnosis of Narcissistic Personality Disorder (NPD) is applied to individuals whose difficulty maintaining self-esteem is manifest in a particular and, to some extent, paradoxical manner. Patients with this designation demonstrate self-aggrandizing and sometimes arrogant behavior, including frequent displays or exaggerations of achievements and accomplishments. Such individuals may also appear vain and preoccupied with their physical appearance and attractiveness. In some cases, the need for admiration or praise is covert and evident only in excessive and apparently self-sacrificing devotion to work or intellectual pursuits. However, a pleasureless driven quality associated with such activities may indicate that they are compulsively pursued in order to maintain or bolster the sense of self.

Self-Sacrifice and the Sense of Self

A thirty-seven-year-old single corporate lawyer came for assessment because she felt "dead," "like an automaton," in spite of a highly successful professional career. As a child, she felt valued only for her academic successes, and as an adult, she felt undesirable to others. It was only in her work that she felt she could provide something of value to others. Because of her ability and her devotion of all of her free time to her work, she had become extremely accomplished in her field. However, she began to feel resentful about being valued only for her work and regretted that she had avoided relationships and other potential sources of personal satisfaction.

_____

Overtly self-sacrificing or grandiose behaviors may derive from the need for admiration or responsiveness from others in order to maintain the sense of self. This need is universal but is particularly great in individuals with a relative deficiency in their own capacity to maintain self-esteem. In some cases, positive and negative feelings about the self are not well integrated. Grandiosity or self-depreciation may then appear together or in an alternating fashion.

Another striking feature of individuals with narcissistic disorders is their relative lack of empathy for others. Empathy, in this context, refers to the ability to understand the feelings and experience of others. A relative deficiency in this ability interferes with the capacity or motivation to attend to emotional and social cues in reciprocal interactions with others. As a result, patients with narcissistic disorders may be insensitive to others, not necessarily out of malice but from a lack of appreciation of their feelings. Such obliviousness to the feelings of others and the consequent lack of depth in relationships may be masked by more superficial sociability. Interactions with others are then based more on learned social cues than on intuitive or empathic understanding.

As a result of insensitivity to others, narcissistic difficulties may create problems in interpersonal relationships even when there is great success in professional or other activities. Distress usually appears only when recognition or praise is not available or when circumstances affect an individual's ability to feel powerful, valued, or attractive. This may occur for a variety of reasons but often follows the physical changes of advancing age or illness or the loss of an important relationship. It may be only when such losses occur that individuals with narcissistic problems seek help.

Physical Illness and Impaired Self-Esteem

A sixty-two-year-old man was president of a successful corporation for many years until he suffered a stroke. He had been a charismatic, attractive individual who was recognized and greatly admired by others. Although self-confident, his self-esteem was maintained and bolstered by the power and appreciation that he derived from his position and from his appealing manner. Unfortunately, his stroke caused him to lose his corporate position and appearance of physical strength. He began to feel inconsolably depressed and worthless and ultimately made a serious suicidal attempt. His underlying difficulty maintaining self-esteem became evident only when the external sources of praise, admiration, and power were lost.

There may have been no evidence of a narcissistic disturbance in this middle-aged man prior to his stroke. His underlying problem regulating self-esteem had not been evident because of the power and admiration that he received from his work, his appearance, and social skills. It was only when he lost some of these attributes that self-doubt and self-denigration emerged.

Self-esteem is affected in most individuals with a major physical illness. However, when there is a preexisting vulnerability in the sense of self, objectively minor changes in social status or physical appearance may be experienced as devastating. Patients with anorexia nervosa and bulimia nervosa demonstrate an inordinate linkage of the sense of self to physical appearance. However, body preoccupation exists on a continuum in the population.

A twenty-two-year-old woman presented with concern about her appearance associated with dieting and binge eating for the preceding two years. She had a childhood history of a learning disability associated with frustration and low self-esteem, but during her teenage years, she had felt admired for her slim, athletic appearance. Unfortunately, mild weight gain had triggered profound anxiety and distress, although this change in her appearance was not evident to anyone else. The vulnerability in her self-esteem only became manifest when she experienced the loss of a physical attribute that she felt to be necessary to sustain her sense of self.

Narcissism and Self-Denigration

In the course of our clinical work, we have observed a group of patients whose narcissistic difficulties are initially manifest not in grandiosity but in self-denigration, self-doubt, or even self-disgust. Such individuals do not believe that they have any characteristic that would be appealing or impressive to others. Paradoxically, the underlying basis for grandiosity and self-denigration may be the same. Further, self-effacing individuals may reveal feelings that they are special in the special consideration to which they may feel entitled.

A thirty-two-year-old professional woman described difficulties in relationships and a fear of letting herself be known to others. She felt profoundly unattractive and was preoccupied with minor physical blemishes and personal defects. It was only late in psychotherapeutic treatment that critical feelings toward others and a wish to be regarded as unique and special to the therapist emerged.

Narcissism and Self-Doubt

Another group of patients with narcissistic problems present with a relative inability to trust their own capacity to think, make decisions, or rely on their own perceptions. These individuals may experience others positively but may easily feel disappointed or disillusioned. They may be prone to turn to therapists or others for "answers" or "cures" and may feel disappointed or enraged when such individuals fail to meet their expectations. To protect themselves from disappointment, such individuals may not let others become important to them, or they may be repeatedly attracted to charismatic figures. They may have difficulty in a therapy in which the therapist's posture is quiet and reflective rather than omnipotent and directive.

A thirty-five-year-old successful academic with a lifelong physical disability sought therapy because he felt inadequate in romantic relationships and experienced chronic dysphoria. Soon after beginning treatment, he began to complain about the absence of improvement. He frequently asked the therapist for advice about life decisions, and he also joined a charismatic quasi-therapeutic movement. He often contrasted the energizing group sessions with the slow process of psychotherapy. Eventually he became a group leader in this movement and terminated his therapy. It appeared that the relatively passive posture of the therapist in this dynamic treatment did not provide a sufficient sense of strength or vitality, and he found the self-reflection imposed by such a treatment to be threatening.

Narcissism and Self-Sufficiency

Some individuals with narcissistic problems appear self-absorbed and devoid of needs because they have closed off such feelings in order to prevent further disappointment or injury. This apparent self-sufficiency may conceal the depth of reliance on connections with others. When they come for treatment, their initial posture is often one of detachment and self-sufficiency.

One patient commented that he did not expect the therapy to be a "collaboration" and preferred the therapist to maintain a friendly but distant posture. However, when such individuals do permit deeper attachments to form, there is often an exquisite sensitivity to feelings of rejection or betrayal.

A man in his thirties came for consultation because of lifelong suicidal impulses, chronic feelings of despair, and an apparent lack of need for others. Despite an abusive childhood, he married, had a child, and had built an extremely successful business. He tended to bolster himself by engaging in exciting, high-risk daredevil pursuits, until an injury prevented him from continuing these activities. He and his wife saw a marital counselor because of tension that began to arise between them. However, when he believed that the counselor, whom he saw individually on several occasions, had revealed some of his intimate confidences to his wife, he felt betrayed and "violated" and ended the therapy. When he saw a new therapist, he found it difficult to trust and was vigilant for any evidence of betrayal by this new therapist. It was only when his sense of betrayal was explored and understood that the treatment could proceed.

ISSUES IN TREATMENT

Most patients with narcissistic disorders do not come for treatment unless they have experienced repeated losses or physical changes that affect their self-esteem. However, some seek treatment because they feel unable to experience deep attachments, because they have hypochondriacal concerns, or because they are sensitive to feelings of injury. Many such patients will benefit most from brief dynamic therapies focused on providing symptomatic relief. A smaller number of such individuals, particularly those who are introspective, psychologically minded, and motivated for insight may benefit from longer-term treatment. Long-term treatment may be open-ended or may have a predetermined duration, as circumstances permit.

Transference and Countertransference

What may be most unique about the psychotherapeutic treatment of patients with significant narcissistic difficulties is the nature of the therapeutic relationships that are formed and the feelings that are evoked in therapists. We have found that in order to treat patients with narcissistic disorders, it is necessary to be comfortable with both the idealizations and critical denunciations of our patients. Sometimes it is necessary to be less active and to accept a relatively passive, quiet, affirming role. Indeed, some patients with narcissistic disorders require us to mirror their insights or their work in the therapy rather than to display our own brilliance. At other times, considerable activity on the part of the therapist is necessary in order to convey interest and engagement. Overall, our responsiveness to the patient's initiatives and needs promotes the unfolding of the patient's own potential.

Working with patients with narcissistic disorders sometimes requires accepting what appear to be unreasonable demands, expectations, or criticisms. We cannot avoid disappointing patients, particularly those whose needs are very specific or exacting. In fact, it is important to understand that the anger that arises during the course of treatment often follows the patient's perception that the therapist has failed to respond adequately to his need for recognition or praise. Patients who require our involvement to maintain their sense of self may be prone to experience disappointment or injury. We may feel unjustly criticized by individuals who continue to feel disappointed or hurt by us in spite of our best efforts. However, although such criticisms can be demoralizing to us, accepting the validity of our patients' feelings, perceptions, and needs may be essential for their development. Indeed, the emergence of these needs must occur in order for therapy to proceed.

Idealization and Disillusionment

A woman who had suffered from a chronic respiratory illness began psychotherapeutic treatment. After several years, her respiratory symptoms had disappeared, but she became preoccupied with the search for stable relationships. She went on a holiday trip with a relative but had a very stormy time with her during the trip. When she returned, she was bitterly disappointed with the therapist for not having warned her that this would happen, and she spent several sessions berating him. The therapist did not ask how he could have known what would happen. He did ask how this made her feel, and he accepted her feelings of bitter disappointment with the lack of guidance and concern that she had experienced from him. It was only much later in the treatment that she came to feel able to trust another person, the therapist, for the first time in her life.

It is sometimes difficult for therapists to appreciate that patients who criticize them may have feelings toward them that are basically positive. Being able to communicate anger to a therapist may actually derive from a basic sense of security that has developed in the treatment.

Basic Positive Transference

A patient repeatedly accused his therapist of various failures, particularly of not caring about him. However, he was astonished when the therapist revealed that he felt that the patient hated him. The patient considered his expressions of anger to be a manifestation of his feelings of openness and trust in the therapist, and he assumed that the therapist would know about his underlying feelings of affection and goodwill.

Although it may be difficult for a therapist to tolerate a patient's relentless anger, it can be even more difficult to tolerate admiration. Admiration may evoke in the therapist fears of intimacy or grandiosity, or concerns that the relationship might be sexualized. Nevertheless, therapists may need to accept such positive feelings from their patients rather than to correct such "unrealistic" beliefs.

When a patient in therapy with one of us in a hospital setting learned that her therapist planned to enter private practice, she believed that the hospital administration must have been quite upset. She stated that his corner office indicated that he must have had a very important position in the institution. This idealization provoked discomfort in the therapist, who hastily pointed out that this corner office had just happened to be available when he arrived and further that it was not even on the main floor where all the other therapists were located. The patient seemed disappointed with this clarification and then seemed more subdued for the rest of the session.

Although motivated by well-intentioned modesty, the therapist's need to disown his own importance caused the patient to feel deflated. If the therapist had been more comfortable with the patient's idealizing feelings, he might have been able to accept rather than to correct the patient's experience. Some practitioners tend not to accept idealizations because they view such feelings as a defense against underlying hostility or contempt. Although idealization may be defensive, it more often reflects a legitimate need of the patient to experience someone important in positive terms. Indeed, individuals who were unable to sustain positive feelings toward a parent because of abuse, absence, or because of the parent's own self-esteem difficulties may present in therapy with prominent idealizing needs.

Permitting these feelings to emerge in therapy may promote development. However, accepting the patient's need to idealize should not be confused with the therapist's requiring such idealizations. In the latter case, the therapist's need to be mirrored imposes a burden on the patient that often interferes with the emergence of the patient's legitimate needs.

COURSE OF TREATMENT

The initial phase of therapy in patients with narcissistic disorders may often be smooth. Such patients may be verbal, witty, and engaging in the treatment sessions. However, in some cases this easy relationship reflects a "pseudo-engagement." If this is not identified and addressed, treatment may proceed smoothly to its termination without any real change having taken place. A lack of depth in a patient's attachment may be manifest by the patient's "forgetting" what happened almost immediately after the sessions or by a lack of feeling about separations from the therapist. One patient in long-term treatment described being unable to remember anything about any session after "hitting the parking lot." A second patient had constructed a psychological "glass bubble" around himself so that he felt disrupted and intruded on when the therapist came to the waiting room to invite him into the office. Such distancing is usually a protection to prevent further injury.

The initial detachment of some patients has sometimes caused us to underestimate their difficulties or to question their suitability for treatment. Indeed, this detachment may be easily misconstrued as a lack of motivation for treatment. However, apparent detachment may reflect not a lack of interest but a need for protection from further injury. Some patients are more engaged than they seem and may demonstrate a great sensitivity to injury by the therapist. We have sometimes not fully appreciated this sensitivity, and our feelings of boredom or restlessness have sometimes been the only clue that a patient has walled off feelings of attachment to prevent injury. Initial difficulties in the therapeutic relationship can also occur when narcissistic patients feel subtly criticized or rejected by therapists who experience them as self-aggrandizing or arrogant. For many, the sense that the therapist is interested in them and their accomplishments is essential in order for treatment to proceed.

Later in treatment, patients may be able to tolerate a broader range of inner feelings and to experience a deeper attachment to the therapist. We have sometimes become aware of this through an increased freedom we have felt to be ourselves with the patient. Paradoxically, some patients may appear less stable after a deep attachment has formed. This apparent worsening may be due to their increased access to their emotional life and to the greater vulnerability to psychological injury within the deeper relationship. At this stage, there may be profound distress when they feel slighted or not valued by us or when blows to their self-esteem arise elsewhere. As treatment progresses, however, the capacity to tolerate injuries of this kind increases and the ability to sustain self-esteem becomes greater. The need for exhibitionistic behavior may then diminish, and these individuals may now be more able to enter into more authentic and meaningful relationships and activities. Goals and ambitions may appear that are now based more on the values and aspirations of the individual than on the need to impress others.

"Curative Factors"

There are many nonspecific factors that are important in the outcome of therapy. These include the predictability, reliability, and nonjudgmental attitude of the therapist. We have found that a number of other factors are also important in the "curative" aspects of the treatment of patients with NPD. We have learned that it is important for the therapist to be cautious about explaining, or correcting the thinking of the patient, or substituting their theories or explanations for those of the patient. In particular, felt experiences including disappointments with the therapist must be acknowledged as real, whether or not we feel unjustly criticized.

Individuals with NPD may already suffer from a lack of trust in their own thinking. We have become aware of how important it is to support and affirm independent thinking on the part of the patient, especially when expressed tentatively. Validation of the patient's thinking and emotional experience is crucial to the growth of new capacities. Our active interest in the patient's experience may facilitate the capacity for self-awareness and self-reflection.

The histories of patients with NPD often reveal a striking paucity of relationships in which parental figures were responsive to them. As a result of these developmental failures, the need to be understood and to have their experience validated and responded to may emerge prominently in therapy. Patients with narcissistic problems often avoid creative or intellectual activities that require initiative because they fear failure or because they lack belief in the validity of such endeavors. Anger that arises in the treatment setting is often secondary to perceived or anticipated failure of the therapist to respond adequately to the patient's need for affirmation, recognition, or praise.

A sign of a successful treatment is the expansion of new areas of interest, enjoyment, accomplishment, or creativity. The development of self-confidence and the sense of support and genuine interest from another may facilitate participation in new activities. At first, the patient may only be able to value such activities when they are recognized and affirmed by the therapist. Therapists may underestimate the importance of these activities to the patient because they are often initially expressed in a muted, tentative, or dismissive fashion. As treatment progresses, the patient may demonstrate less need for the therapist to be interested in or to affirm their interests in order for them to initiate, pursue, or enjoy them.

The issue of disillusionment is often a critical one in the treatment of patients with narcissistic disorders. In some cases, there is a history of intense idealization and subsequent painful disillusionment with those with whom they become involved. A more gradual process of disillusionment with the therapist may reflect growth and development during the course of therapy. Such disillusionment needs to be understood or accepted without defensiveness by the therapist and is likely to be accompanied in the patient by increased self-reliance and trust in their own ideas and by a decreased need to rely on the opinions and ideas of others. When the patient's disillusionment is too intense or premature, the therapy may be disrupted and profound feelings of hopelessness may emerge.

While the treatment of patients with NPD may be lengthy and stormy, the results can be exceptionally rewarding. What may occur is not merely symptomatic relief but a significant change in the individual's capacity to feel authentic, to engage in meaningful life pursuits, to experience empathy for others, and to form rewarding and sustaining relationships. For example, a patient who began long-term treatment had been perceived as controlling and arrogant. The therapist initially felt irritated by this patient's condescending attitude, but he later came to understand that what underlay the patient's attitude were feelings of vulnerability, loneliness, and insecurity. An accepting and nondefensive attitude of the therapist allowed these feelings to emerge. Toward the end of the treatment, the patient revealed that while he had previously felt no possibility for happiness, he now tended to regard himself as lucky and to count his blessings. He said that this change had started when he had noticed a change in the therapist and had begun to feel that the therapist could like him and could support his own interests and initiatives.

FOR FURTHER READING

Adler, G. (1981). The borderline-narcissistic continuum. *American Journal of Psychiatry, 138*, 46–50.

Akhtar, S. (1989). Narcissistic personality disorders: Descriptive features and differential diagnosis. *Psychiatric Clinics of North America, 12*, 505–529.

Baker, H. S., & Baker, M. N. (1987). Heinz Kohut's self psychology: An overview. *American Journal of Psychiatry, 144*, 1–9.

Goldberg, A. (1989). Self psychology and the narcissistic personality disorder. *Psychiatric Clinics of North America, 12*, 731–739.

Kernberg, O. (1989). The narcissistic personality disorder and the differential diagnosis of antisocial behavior. *Psychiatric Clinics of North America, 12*, 553–570.

Kohut, H. (1984). *How does analysis cure?* Chicago: University of Chicago Press.

Lasch, C. (1978). *The culture of narcissism: American life in an age of diminishing expectations.* New York: Norton.

Reich, A. (1960). Pathologic forms of self-esteem regulation. *Psychoanalytical Study of the Child, 15*, 215–232.

6

ASSESSMENT AND MANAGEMENT OF ANTISOCIAL PERSONALITY DISORDER

Robert G. Ruegg, Caroline Haynes, and Allen Frances

The concept of Antisocial Personality Disorder (ASPD) is not a new one, though the diagnostic criteria used to define the disorder have changed with time. Terms like *psychopath*, *sociopath*, *dyssocial personality*, *criminal personality*, and now *antisocial personality* have all been used to describe a type of character who repeatedly breaks the law and misuses other people in the heat of passion, or for amusement, or for personal gain, and often without remorse. Criminal behavior, but not necessarily violent criminal behavior, is usually part of the syndrome.

Some controversy exists about whether we should label people with these problems with a psychiatric diagnosis or simply consider them "bad." Since we do not have much to offer in the way of proven, effective treatment for ASPD, one could argue against the value of considering this a psychiatric diagnosis. However, recent studies of risk factors for a person developing antisocial personality show that there are both inherited and environmental factors that are important, lending hope that eventually some combination of biological and psychosocial treatments may be more helpful than current interventions. Other studies showing that some antisocial characters "burn out" in midlife and become more law abiding encourage us to find ways to speed this process along. This population is a tough one to work with, but most of us will encounter these individuals in the course of our practice.

This chapter is intended to help clinicians in their assessment and management of ASPD. It will address assessment techniques, treatment options, risks of treatment, and legal and ethical issues in the treatment of this population.

Since the diagnosis of antisocial personality is made far more often in men, we will describe our hypothetical patient as "he" instead of "he or she" for the sake of making the material more accessible. But the reader should keep in mind that women may also suffer from this problem.

ASSESSMENT AND DIAGNOSIS

Current diagnostic criteria for Antisocial Personality Disorder in the *DSM-IV* system require that the person have "an enduring pattern of behavior that deviates markedly from the expectations of the individual's culture." The pattern should be obvious in many life situations (home, work, social activity) and should cause significant distress to self or others or impairment. It should not be caused by another mental disorder or medical problem. It should not be solely the result of drug use or abuse. The specific feature of Antisocial Personality Disorder that distinguishes it from other personality disorders is that the person has a pattern of disregard for and violation of the rights of others since at least age fifteen. This means that the person habitually:

- Breaks the law
- Is deceitful and lies
- Is impulsive
- Is aggressive
- Is reckless

- Is irresponsible
- Lacks remorse, or doesn't care, or rationalizes what harm he has done

The presence of three of these behaviors at a level of clinically significant impairment is enough for the diagnosis. If the extent of these behaviors is less impairing or if they are limited only to certain parts of a person's life, a diagnosis of "Antisocial Personality Traits" can be made. The diagnostic criteria set of the *International Classification of Diseases (ICD-10) for Antisocial Personality Disorder* stresses criminal behavior less and lack of remorse more than the *DSM-IV* set.

Childhood Conduct Disorder is a necessary precursor to adult Antisocial Personality Disorder, which has similar diagnostic criteria. Children and adolescents with this problem also show behaviors in which the rights of others or social norms are violated. They exhibit aggression toward people and animals, destroy property, lie, steal, and break rules at home and in school. Although the criteria for ASPD require problems since age fifteen, a much earlier onset implies higher risk and greater severity.

One distinction that has been lost in the *DSM-IV* criteria is that of solitary versus group aggressive behavior—in other words, does the child or adolescent act aggressively by himself or only in the company of and out of loyalty to peers, as in a gang? There is some evidence to suggest that the group aggressive type has a better prognosis, perhaps because new loyalties can be formed.

In the current United States population, it is estimated that 3 percent of men and 1 percent of women qualify for the antisocial personality diagnosis. Six to 16 percent of male adolescents and 2 to 9 percent of female adolescents are conduct-disordered. These percentages are higher than in Norwegian populations where only 0.1 percent of men have ASPD. Lower socioeconomic status and urban locations are associated with these diagnoses. Despite having the same diagnosis, women with this disorder more often meet the criteria because of nonviolent behavior like forgery, fraud, or theft, and men because of violent behavior such as assault, rape, or murder. By current criteria, about 80 percent of prison inmates have Antisocial Personality Disorder. Of course, the majority of persons with the disorder are not imprisoned.

Portrait of the Patient with Antisocial Personality Disorder

The life of the patient with Antisocial Personality Disorder is characterized by a chronic pattern of poor role performance as a citizen, on the job, or as a spouse or parent. Violation of the rights of others, anger, violence, and substance abuse are characteristic. He may come to the attention of mental health care providers for dangerous (suicidal or homicidal) talk or behavior. He may come feigning physical or psychological symptoms in order get some drug to abuse, to evade responsibility for some crime, or to get disability benefits, or even just to get food, clothing, and shelter. We may encounter him in private counseling offices, at mental health centers, in hospitals, or in jails.

As mentioned earlier, a history of conduct disorder starting before age fifteen is essential to the diagnosis. Girls tend to start having symptoms of conduct disorder later than boys do. If the patient was already in trouble in elementary school, this is a sign that his problems will be especially severe and persistent. He does not like his life. He experiences a lot of dysphoria, tension, boredom, depression, and anger. When he is young, he feels this is because he doesn't get the right breaks and because he is being victimized. As he gets older, he often starts to realize that he himself has something to do with the misery he experiences. He often tends to get better with time. But as he remits, the antisocial behaviors are often replaced with depressive and somatic disorders.

At night in the emergency room, he will tell you he will commit suicide or kill someone else unless you admit him to the hospital. You may feel personally threatened and intimidated, even if he is not overtly targeting you with his aggressive ideas. By admitting him, you may seem to be caving in to his threats and reinforcing his manipulative behavior. But he may really act on his threats. Sometimes he will do it for no other reason than just to prove to you that he will. He is usually drunk or high at the time. Eighty percent of patients with Antisocial Personality Disorder abuse drugs or alcohol. The already high risk of suicide or homicide is further elevated when he is intoxicated. Antisocial Personality Disorder should come to mind any time you have to deal with a drunk (or otherwise intoxicated) and dangerous patient.

Getting a history of repeated recklessness, dangerousness, or suicidality with or without intoxication is a good clue to the diagnosis of Antisocial Personality Disorder. Also, this is a reason to hope that he will no longer harbor these ideas next morning when he has sobered up or when he has simply "gotten over" his tantrum. As with borderlines, the only thing predictable is change. And change usually takes a few minutes, hours, or at most, days. No matter how irascible and impossible to evaluate the fellow is on the night of admission, the next morning, or the day after that, he may be as pleasant and cooperative as any other patient. Until the next "tantrum."

The Psychopath Versus the Impulsive Antisocial Personality

The *DSM-IV* criteria for ASPD probably capture a heterogeneous sample. It may eventually be subtyped based on personality features. Although 80 percent of prisoners have ASPD, only 10 to 30 percent of patients with Antisocial Personality Disorder have what has been called psychopathy. Psychopathy has been suggested as a distinct subtype of ASPD whose members are cold and remorseless. It was, in fact, described before ASPD in the 1950s by Cleckley in *The Mask of Sanity*. The current diagnostic criteria are more inclusive. They describe both the remorseless Cleckley psychopath and the more typical unstable and impulsive antisocial character who is more likely to feel remorse. It is worthwhile to be able to recognize these suggested types as different because their prognoses in treatment may be different.

The impulsive but remorseful antisocial character has serious impulse control problems and acts, often aggressively, in the heat of passion or the thrill of the moment. He enjoys taking risks and is prospectively undaunted by the possibility of bad consequences. In some ways, he is like a child who acts impulsively and does not yet have wisdom, or respect for consequences, or a built-in conscience. Like a child, he may even want to behave better and, when out of control, may want external limits set on his behavior. When incarcerated, he may become a model prisoner. He will, of course, then earn an early release. On the outside again, without the external controls and supervision he will, like a three-year-old, soon return to mischief.

He is more sophisticated than a child, though, and has usually learned better ways to avoid guilt by blaming someone or something else for his misdeeds. He has often learned that there are rewards for misbehavior, too. He may in time do antisocial things in a more planned, less impulsive way for some personal gain. For example, he may learn that physically threatening behavior "works" to get what he wants and may use it even when he's not angry.

The Cleckley psychopath, on the other hand, is slicker and more deliberate from the start. His motivation for violence will not be acute anger or jealousy or raging lust but calculated retribution, simmering revenge, or personal gain. His antisocial acts are often carefully planned. They are executed with a triumphant sense of satisfaction and cool entitlement. He will make you an intimidating "offer you can't refuse." He may be quite charming and convincing. He will be without loyalty and remorse, but will probably have a good act and a remarkable ability to gain your confidence.

He is more likely to have an education and very high social status than the impulsive type. He is more prone to have co-morbid Histrionic and Narcissistic Personality Disorders or traits. He may believe he is unique and therefore above the law, and may expect admiration for his crimes. He feels entitled to casual, callous exploitation of anyone he encounters—including you and the health care system. He is less likely to respond to efforts to rehabilitate him and is more likely to return to prison. Because his behavior is more deliberate and disguised and less impulsive, it is even harder to diagnose the patient with psychopathy than the one with impulsive Antisocial Personality Disorder who can barely restrain himself.

In summary, you could say that the violent impulsive antisocial personality is "just out of control." The violent psychopath, on the other hand, is "just taking care of business."

Psychopathic Psychotic Disorder

An even rarer and more malignant subtype of Antisocial Personality Disorder is called Psychopathic Psychotic Disorder. It was first described by Robert Srna in 1995. These individuals may make up only 1 to 2 percent of patients with Antisocial Personality Disorder. They are slovenly in their appearance and grooming. Even the other psychopaths regard them as "losers." They have even less regard for their own or others' safety, and even in prison they are always in trouble. Their hallucinations sound like morbid fantasies about killing or mutilating themselves or others, which they act out. They do not improve with typical antipsychotic drugs but do seem to respond to risperidone.

The Assessment Interview

One of your most important jobs is to assess the risk of suicide or homicide. At the start of the interview, ask a new or unwilling patient if you will be in any danger while you interview him. You will put the "tough-guy" patient at ease when he realizes you are suitably impressed by his potential dangerousness. You may see him relax and lean back in his chair. But if he has recently been violent, seems agitated or restless, or the setting is an emergency room, ask security personnel to keep an eye on the two of you.

A history of violence is one of the few valid indicators we have for predicting future violence. Ask about this. "Do you have a history of violence or of trying to hurt yourself?" will do the trick. Many will tell you if they do. But don't assume a "No" answer is truthful. Assume he is dangerous if during a stress- or drug-induced micropsychotic episode he is having auditory hallucinations that command him to be violent to himself or others. Is he hypervigilant, seeming to expect and be ready for an attack? Observe him for agitation or restlessness. This indicates his current state of arousal and readiness to act. Is there a friend or family member who can tell you what he is likely to do in this state or who is willing and able to supervise him until the danger subsides? If you don't feel comfortable that any dangerousness is under control, you should consider a period of emergency room observation or a brief hospitalization while he calms down.

You can use your own feelings as an assessment tool. Pay attention to your feelings when you are with the patient. Do you feel vaguely threatened or intimidated? Are you afraid not to give him what he seems to want? Do you suspect you are being used, perhaps to get some drug or to give him an excuse for some misbehavior? Do you feel contemptuous or hostile and irritable? Do you have fantasies of punishing or persecuting him or putting him in his place? Do you want to do him a favor? Or even rescue him? Are you being seduced? Do you feel sexually attracted or threatened? Do you feel he is coolly disregarding your authority as a professional? Does he seem incongruously cool and nonchalant about the interview and his present difficulties? Does his eye contact seem a little too steady, as if he is appraising you? Or does his gaze seem superficial, as if he were looking right through you? Or is his eye contact inappropriately increased, as if he were deliberately trying to convey sincerity and elicit your confidence in himself? These can all be signs that you are dealing with a patient with Antisocial Personality Disorder.

If you know that the person you are interviewing has anti-social personality or traits, keep in mind that the information you are going to get is not likely to be accurate. The patient may have something to hide and may also enjoy tricking and manipulating you. He will be sizing you up for what you can do for him and how he can control or intimidate you. It is a good idea to tell him that you expect to be taken in at times by his deceptions, that this is a symptom of his disorder. This can convey to him that you accept him despite his disease. It will also reduce his contempt for you when he does take you in, because you predicted it. In the outpatient setting, you may not know the diagnosis in advance. Here you must pay attention to your own sense of feeling threatened, uneasy, or duped to raise your index of suspicion about this diagnosis. A story that seems vague or evasive or that changes between interviews or interviewers is a clue to habitual lying, another criterion for diagnosis. Bragging about reckless, "macho" behavior is a another clue to the diagnosis. If you let him brag and perhaps let him believe you are curious or impressed, you may be able to elicit more information about his exploits.

You can start a psychosocial history interview with usually innocuous questions to put him at ease. Ask where he was born and raised and about his childhood. He may say something that lets you know whether he habitually blames others for bad things in his life. How did he get along with his peers and teachers in elementary school? Ask about his junior high school years. It is important to ask about suspensions, starting fights, truancy, running away, and other symptoms of conduct disorder. If you don't, you may never know you are dealing with a patient with Antisocial Personality Disorder. In that case, your treatment and treatment expectations will be frustrated because they will be inappropriate to the case.

Of course, the more sophisticated the patient is, the more he will be able to conceal socially undesirable aspects of his past history from you—or at least cast them in a better light. If he feels you might think his exploits are at least understandable or perhaps even forgivable, he will be likely to tell you more. To fill out the picture he paints, you need to check collateral history from family, friends, the referral source, or even his criminal record.

Differential Diagnosis

Diagnosing Antisocial Personality Disorder or traits is not difficult *if you have the requisite information*, since the criteria listed earlier are not ambiguous. However, when the patient has symptoms of an Axis I disorder as well, the situation is much more complex. In this situation, you must decide:

- Whether the patient has Antisocial Personality Disorder at all or if he has another disorder masquerading as Antisocial Personality Disorder
- Whether the patient has another psychiatric disorder in addition to Antisocial Personality Disorder (co-morbidity)
- Whether the patient is feigning or exaggerating symptoms of another psychiatric disorder because of Antisocial Personality Disorder

The patient with Antisocial Personality Disorder often claims to have an Axis I major mental illness. He may hope that this will protect him from responsibility for his misbehaviors. He may be running a scam to get food, clothing, shelter, or disability benefits. He may understandably be trying to avoid the pejorative connotations that the diagnosis of Antisocial Personality Disorder carries even with some members of the mental health field. Having a patient with a diagnosis of Antisocial Personality Disorder is a good reason to suspect that he is malingering symptoms of other psychiatric diseases. Many of these patients are authorities on the *DSM* criteria for the disorder they are dissembling. Others have carefully observed their mentally ill peers while in the hospital. Put off making an early diagnosis. Get collateral history. See if inconsistencies appear on repeat interviews.

Nevertheless, Axis I psychiatric illness is in fact more common in patients with Antisocial Personality Disorder than it is in the general population. He is more likely to have Major Depression, Bipolar Illness, Panic Disorder, Posttraumatic Stress Disorder, Attention Deficit Disorder, or learning disabilities. We will consider these possibilities for some commonly co-morbid Axis I illnesses.

Major Depression. Patients with Antisocial Personality Disorder have mood changes that are just as severe as those of patients with the usual mood disorders. However, the time course is often different, and the mood is most often anger. A depressed mood swing in a patient with Antisocial Personality Disorder may only last a few minutes or hours. This is the same length of time that moods last in any of us. But in the patient with Antisocial Personality Disorder, the intensity of the mood is much greater. The ashen color, hunched shoulders, suicidal ideas, and psychomotor retardation can be just as severe for those with Major Depression. But these biological signs of depression can clear as rapidly as they appeared. On the other hand, probably 30 percent of patients with Antisocial Personality Disorder eventually do get Major Depression, usually after age thirty or thirty-five. You may be able to tell because the patient will have the same glum expression, when not distracted, for the majority of most days for over two weeks. However, this is usually an atypical or "reactive" depression, in that he brightens up when you approach. Unlike melancholic depressives, he can also be drawn into some interesting or distracting activity. Because of this affective responsiveness, it may be hard to believe his reports of depression are not bogus. But the key difference is his uncharacteristic passivity. He will no longer initiate things on his own.

Here is a story of a patient with Antisocial Personality Disorder who presented with Major Depression:

BILL

Bill, forty-five, was a "frequent flyer" at the state hospital and a shrewd operator. We first got to know him when he was not depressed; however, he would usually claim he was depressed and suicidal. He came in when he was drunk and dangerous but did not want to go to jail. In the hospital, he would make himself comfortable. He would somehow come up with piles of candy and other goodies and sell them to other patients on the ward, against the rules, at a handsome profit. A $200 wad of one-dollar bills was found on him on one occasion during a resuscitation from a faked suicide attempt.

Once, however, he got tens of thousands of dollars in an insurance settlement involving a traffic accident (fraudulently, no doubt). Unfortunately for him and fortunately for his dealer, he spent it all in a six-week cocaine binge. Afterward, he had to sober up and realize what he had done. That's when he became depressed. The staff who had known him from all his previous admissions observed that he did seem different this time. He wasn't always trying to run a scam or get around the ward rules. When approached, he would still respond with eye contact and a bright affect; he would still play cards with the guys if asked. But he would no longer initiate any of these things. If not approached, he would sit with a downcast gaze for long periods of time or stay in his room.

If you think your patient has Major Depression, you should consider pharmacotherapy. The lifetime suicide risk of 5 to 10 percent for individuals with antisocial personality is likely due in part to the high rate of untreated depression.

Recent studies have shown that perhaps 30 percent of men with Major Depression have rage attacks. Rage attacks are also characteristic of Antisocial Personality Disorder, so we have to be alert enough to think of this. Depressed men may not even experience a depressed mood or call themselves depressed. They may only have unexplained pain or somatic syndromes or have lost interest in things they used to care about and have some other signs of depression like disturbed sleep, energy, or appetite. If they have been depressed and have been having rage attacks for years, they may have alienated their families, who have come to regard them as dangerous antisocial characters. But their families will be able to remember when they were not so grouchy and irritable and prone to violent outbursts. These rage attacks will go away when the depression is diagnosed and treated.

Bipolar Disorder. Among the traits of Manic Depressive Illness are impulsivity, grandiosity, and entitlement. These patients feel entitled to all that is coming to them and to all that is coming to you, too. They are often very persuasive, manipulative, histrionic, and seductive, just as patients with Antisocial Personality Disorder are. They will be hypersexual and assume that you will be delighted to be sexual with them. For these sorts of reasons, patients with Bipolar Disorder will often end up in jail along with persons with Antisocial Personality Disorder.

Once in jail, they will not be too hard to spot. They will usually have been high functioning before they got sick and will not have the typical air of a street person. They will not sleep and will restlessly pace their cells and will talk endlessly and rapidly. This can go on for minutes to hours with Antisocial Personality Disorder, but it continues for days and weeks in mania. They need pharmacotherapy. Patients with Antisocial Personality Disorder and co-morbid Bipolar Disorder may also learn to use the Axis I disorder to explain their behavior, as in this vignette:

SAM

Sam was a thirty-five-year-old man with well-known, lithium-responsive Bipolar Disorder and a very positive family history for Bipolar Disorder and antisocial personality. He became irritable, combative, and impulsively aggressive when manic. Between episodes of illness, he engaged in a variety of petty property crimes and habitually lied to family members about his finances, debts, and whereabouts. When they confronted him or set limits on their support, he became enraged and would try to make them feel to blame and guilty about his illness, while acting helpless and pouting. After seeing his family's response to his threatening physical behavior, he learned to use this behavior even while not manic to try to get his way, claiming that he was suddenly manic. He began to make vague verbal and physical threats toward his female therapist and to report manic symptoms that were not consistent with his family's reports or his mental status during sessions.

This turned out to be a tactic intended to get prescriptions for benzodiazepines. His feigning sudden "attacks" of mania didn't stop until the therapist advised the family to call the police when he repeatedly threatened his mother. By the time the police arrived, he was calm and contrite. His threatening behavior stopped completely when his therapist warned that she would terminate therapy if she continued to feel threatened and his mother told him he would have to move out if he destroyed her property.

Panic Disorder, Social Phobia, Posttraumatic Stress Disorder, and Other Anxiety Disorders. These disorders are surprisingly common in patients with Antisocial Personality Disorder. If these symptoms do not respond well to exposure therapy or cognitive-behavior therapy, you should consider pharmacotherapy augmentation. Again, benzodiazepines should not be given to these patients. Antidepressants take longer to give relief but are just as effective as benzodiazepines. Anxiety symptoms may often be feigned to gain sympathy or drugs.

Substance Abuse. Aggressive and reckless uninhibited behavior is seen in patients with either substance abuse or Antisocial Personality Disorder. As we said before, nearly all patients with

Antisocial Personality Disorder will have substance abuse, too. Thus, one should always have both diagnoses in mind while making a differential diagnosis of such behavior.

The person with a substance use disorder alone will likely have had a period of pretty normal functioning before the drug got the best of him. He will have a job and family, or at least the memory of it, to return to. He will have a good chance of staying sober for a while after a drug rehabilitation program. His antisocial behavior will often be linked in time and motivation to drug-seeking behavior. Not so with Antisocial Personality Disorder. The person with true Antisocial Personality Disorder will have had problems since his teens or earlier. He will have had little chance to develop personal resources like job skills, a career, reliable friends, a family of his own, or a home. And he will be reckless indefinitely (or at least until middle age) even after being deprived of drugs. His substance abuse will likely relapse sooner after completing a drug rehabilitation program.

In the long-term substance abuser, reckless behavior can become habitual, spreading into his sober life. Thus, substance abusers will be rather impulsive and reckless for months even after sobering up. This is called a "dry drunk." It is one reason recovery from substance abuse takes so long. Thus, Alcoholics Anonymous has a slogan recommending "ninety meetings in ninety days" to newly sober drunks.

As mentioned earlier, 80 percent of patients with Antisocial Personality Disorder will also have substance abuse. The co-morbid substance abuse can significantly worsen the personality disorder symptoms by disinhibiting behavior, contributing to denial, and fueling the need to commit antisocial acts to support the drug habit. Violence, including suicide and homicide, is much more likely when such a person is intoxicated.

Respectful but appropriately pointed queries must be made. "How much do you drink? How often? What kind of trouble have you gotten into while drinking? What other drugs do you use? Marijuana? Cocaine? Crack? What else?" You should assume that substance abuse is present until proved otherwise. It is reasonable and proper to ask the patient to give urine for drug testing. Refer him to a dedicated substance abuse treatment program if his troubles are growing worse from drug use and he doesn't stop using.

Apparent Personality Disorder in Intermittent Explosive Disorder.   Rage attacks are characteristic of patients with Intermittent Explosive Disorder. An irritable or touchy temperament is often the baseline state for these people, as it is in ASPD. They will often do something as outrageous during a rage attack as a patient with Antisocial Personality Disorder would do. They often report the same "seeing red" and partial amnesia for their violent behavior during the episode. But by definition, the rest of their lives will not meet criteria for Antisocial Personality Disorder. They will also typically have remorse and self-reproach for their actions. They will accept responsibility for their destructive behavior and be able to empathize with the people they have hurt. They will want your help in preventing future outbursts. Antidepressants seem to show promise in reducing the severity and frequency of their outbursts.

MANAGEMENT OF ANTISOCIAL PERSONALITY DISORDER

Antisocial Personality Disorder is notoriously resistant to treatment. There are no tried-and-true, proven treatments based on well-controlled studies, though some treatments may help some individuals at least for a time. However, a significant number of antisocial characters (perhaps 30 to 40 percent) will "burn out" in middle age and become less impulsive and violent, or even "reform" by adopting new value systems or religious beliefs. The prison system is recognizing this and now more often releases previously violent criminals in their later years because of decreased risk of harm to others. This "burnout" phenomenon means the situation is not totally hopeless and that some way of promoting this process may be found.

Obstacles to Treatment

A major problem in treating the antisocial patient is that despite the limits that society imposes on antisocial behavior, he may continue to find reward in behaving this way, even in prison. As long as the behavior gets him what he wants, whether it be a thrill, admiration, or material gain, motivation for treatment will suffer. However, prisons provide the most structured environment available for these individuals and may be the most viable setting in which to conduct treatment. It is difficult for the outpatient therapist to detect antisocial behavior that occurs in the patient's life outside therapy and even harder to find ways to change reinforcements for that behavior. At least in prison these behaviors may be detected more often, and reinforcers and punishments are available. Another problem is that whatever treatment you offer, it or you may be abused for another purpose so that the treatment is never really tried as intended.

Perhaps the biggest obstacle to treatment is the offensiveness of such patients' behavior. This offensive behavior can be seen as either "bad" or "sick." In fact, it is often both. "Justice" can take the form of punishment, retribution, or containment. Justice may motivate the person with ASPD to see the badness or sickness of his behavior and to be open to treatment.

Despite these major obstacles, most of us will be called on to evaluate and treat people with antisocial traits or personality at some time. Often we get into this unwittingly and discover the diagnosis only after treatment has begun. It is extremely important to recognize your own attitudes, fears, and limitations in dealing with these people. If these stand in the way of respecting the person or caring for your own needs, the patient should be referred to someone who is more comfortable with this pathology. This is a population that not every therapist is equipped to handle; knowing one's capacities from the outset will help avoid harm to both therapist and patient.

General Considerations in Treatment

The first important decision following diagnosis of a patient with Antisocial Personality Disorder is whether or not to treat. With most disorders, diagnosis implies treatment. The lack of convincing outcome data and the risks of harm to the therapist or patient in this disorder make the decision to treat difficult but important. Factors that weigh in favor of undertaking treatment might include:

- The presence of an Axis I disorder, especially substance use and mood disorder. Because these disorders are often quite treatable and may worsen antisocial behavior, it is usually worth addressing them in treatment.
- High motivation on the patient's part. He may be dissatisfied with his lifestyle or have experienced or anticipate especially negative consequences that provide motivation.
- An external structure that can help monitor behavior and provide reinforcement for positive behavior. This could be a prison or institutional setting, or there may be family who can participate in treatment.
- A history of some positive relationships in the patient's life. This may indicate a capacity to form an alliance with the therapist.
- Antisocial behavior that is impulsive and/or accompanied by any regret, remorse, or negative self-judgment. This may indicate a capacity to be motivated to develop impulse control.
- A desire to live outside jail. In contrast, when a patient has come to depend on an institution for basic life support, he may be motivated to continue antisocial acts in order to maintain this secondary gain.

If such encouraging factors are not present, initiating treatment may not be warranted or should be undertaken only as a brief trial, with clear criteria for termination.

The treatment of antisocial characters is a challenging and often frustrating endeavor. It should not be undertaken by the inexperienced therapist without adequate supervision and support. Treating these patients can result in actual harm to the therapist. It can be physical, as the result of threat or assault. It can be emotional, as the result of being manipulated or feeling a sense of failure. Many features of this personality type fly right in the face of involvement in treatment. These patients are impulsive and act out in therapy. They often quit treatment or participate irregularly. They see the therapist as someone to be manipulated for their own needs. The therapist may become a convenient person to blame when they are enraged or in trouble. Any limits set on the therapeutic situation will be tested and violated.

The therapist had better think in advance about how to deal with such behaviors. Threatening behavior, demands for lending money or writing prescriptions, sexual propositions, and violating rules about phone calls or unannounced visits can be expected. So the therapist needs to set clear, firm, but not punitive limits. Since these patients are impulsive (and often not aware of their motivation for an act beyond "I felt like it"), limits should be set in terms of behavior, not principle. It is better to tell the patient, "I will stop treating you if you steal from my office," rather than "you must respect my property." Certain limits should be automatically built in to the treatment of these patients. For example, they should not be seen in isolated settings or during "off hours." Help should be readily available in case a patient becomes assaultive. The therapist should be ready to remove him- or herself from a session when acutely threatened or from the treatment contract if feeling persistently threatened. No therapist can be effective in setting limits or confronting behavior while feeling threatened. Since she may be considered "easy prey," a female therapist should carefully consider whether she wants to undertake the therapy of a male antisocial patient. Here is an example:

JOHN

John was a thirty-eight-year-old man who came for psychiatric evaluation for depression. He had a full spectrum of depressive symptoms in the wake of his wife "kicking him out for hitting the kids." He was referred to a female therapist for treatment of Major Depression and Narcissistic/Antisocial Personality Disorder. In early sessions, he complained about his wife and resisted any attempt to get him to own part of the problem. He talked a lot about his guns, his history of fighting anyone who challenged him, and what he would like to do to his wife. Though his therapist clarified his lack of intent to follow through on his fantasies at each session, she began to feel increasingly uneasy and anxious before sessions with him.

During the fourth session, the patient wore athletic shorts and adopted a casual posture that resulted in exposing his genitals. He seemed aware but not disturbed by this, while the therapist felt awkward and threatened. When she finally asked him to cover himself, the patient grinned and stated he was sorry if he was bothering her. When he exposed himself again at the next session, the therapist excused herself, asked a male colleague to chaperone the session, and gave the patient the option of continuing in treatment with her in the presence of a male chaperone or of being referred to a male therapist. He chose to be referred and, soon after, dropped out of therapy.

Setting Realistic Expectations

The most critical factor to work on early in treatment is developing an acknowledgment on the patient's part that change is really needed. If we think of antisocial personality as the best adaptation to reality that a person has been able to make given their temperamental characteristics and the learning they have done so far, we can understand that the patient may need some convincing even to imagine that any other adaptation would be better. Emphasizing the negative consequences of antisocial acts (jail, fines, punishment) can help raise this question for the patient. But if the environment continues to reward antisocial behavior (for example, if the patient feels his ability to succeed in prison depends on manipulating the system) and in the face of the patient's inability to experience guilt or shame, it is unlikely that there will be much motivation for change.

In undertaking the therapy of such a patient, the therapist must set expectations realistically and recognize that incentives must be created for change to occur. For patients who are capable of enjoying human contact, regular contact with the nonjudgmental therapist who expresses interest in the patient may be an initial incentive. Even so, the therapist should not expect the patient to feel badly about using, devaluing, or manipulating the therapist, though contact is desired. It is up to the therapist to look out for himself or herself in this regard. Inpatient settings and prisons may offer specific privileges or removal of restrictions as possible incentives, but in outpatient settings, family, school, or other structures may have to be involved in the creation of incentives for change. These incentives may have to persist for a long time, since the patient will not be capable of experiencing a need for change on the basis of internal values for a long time, if ever. The best we may be able to expect as an internalized rationale for change can be summed up as "things go better for me and I get what I need more of the time if I do things differently."

Getting Started

Once some incentives have been created for the patient to consider making changes, specific changes that could be made can be identified. Then the pros and cons of making these changes can be weighed. Antisocial characters, especially the younger ones, may feel that they are giving up a lot to change their intimidating, manipulative, or aggressive behavior. Their view of themselves may depend on these characteristics. They must be able to see that a longer-term gain outweighs the loss in order to have the motivation to try to change. Although the impulse control and judgment of the patient may resemble those of a child, you should not make the mistake of thinking that being attached to or identified with you as an authority figure has any appeal for the antisocial patient as it would for a normal child.

Though you might not agree with the choices made, you should respect the autonomy of the patient in deciding what to change. You can of course set limits on your own involvement with the patient depending on the choices made—for example, you may choose not to see a patient in your outpatient office if the patient does not agree to try to stop stealing from patients in the waiting room! Once the two of you have targeted behaviors for change, the factors maintaining or provoking those behaviors can be identified, and work can begin on reducing those factors and developing alternative behaviors.

Dealing with Aggressive Behavior

Aggressive or assaultive behavior is often one of the first behaviors targeted for change. A cognitive approach can be used here to help the patient value having control of himself instead of being a tough guy. It is important to recognize and identify the positive rewards that patients get from these behaviors and not to assume that this behavior is simply impulsive. Aggression may be used defensively, to maintain a sense of safety, identity, or control. The release of tension associated with outwardly aggressive acts may be very pleasurable, perhaps even addictive. So the patient may be giving up a major coping strategy and a source of gratification by limiting aggressive outbursts. Needless to say, he needs some attractive incentives to convince him that this is worth doing. The patient needs to begin to believe that things might go better for him if this behavior were diminished. Then, the first step toward change is to identify and keep track of when aggression occurs. This can be done by the patient or an observer (parent, ward staff, prison guard) and then used to help the patient identify any triggers or pattern to the behavior that is predictable or avoidable.

Patients may experience that outbursts "just happen" without any awareness of the tension leading up to the outburst. They may benefit from some education about the physiology of anger and some training in recognizing the physical sensations (flushing, heat, clenched fists) or cognitions ("I could kill this guy") associated with anger. Once the patient can identify that an outburst is likely to occur, alternative strategies for dealing with the tension need to be identified and practiced. These could include directing aggression at inanimate objects, verbal rather than physical aggression, relaxation techniques, self-statements, exercise, or complaining to a third party. Imagining violent acts is a technique useful for overinhibited patients. In the underinhibited patient with ASPD, it should probably be avoided, as it may lead to acting them out.

In patients who seem to have high levels of autonomic arousal as a backdrop to outbursts, antisympathetic drugs (beta-blockers, neuroleptics) may have some utility. Some aggressive patients seem to have deficits in the inhibitory serotonergic function in the brain, and serotonergic drugs like the selective serotonin reuptake inhibitors (SSRIs) or lithium may be helpful in reducing anger and aggression. Much more controversial is the treatment of male patients who exhibit sexually violent behavior: they may have a reduction in such behavior with anti-androgenic treatments such as Depo-Provera injections.

Issues in Ongoing Treatment

If the antisocial character can persist in therapy long enough to learn that the therapist will remain if not threatened and that alternatives to threatening behavior can result in some reward, the patient may be able to begin to make use of the therapist in a different way. He may become curious about how the therapist does things (as opposed to truly identifying). Although this may be gratifying (and a relief!) to the therapist and seem like a breakthrough, it is important to keep in mind that the patient may begin to develop significant depression and hopelessness as he becomes aware of the quality of his previous life. If this is not addressed, the patient may sense no choice but to adopt old ways of seeking gratification.

This may be a phase when peer support from other antisocial characters who are dealing with the same sense of loss and hollowness may be especially helpful. Help him find alternative answers to existential questions (new relationships, spiritual/religious activity, educational endeavors, even limited volunteer work) to help fill the void. He may need antidepressant medication.

This phase of treatment may be more likely to be achieved in young patients whose behavior patterns are not so well established and in older patients whose aggression and impulsivity have "burned out," leaving room for an awareness of other possibilities. The therapist must try to maintain the proper balance of support during this phase, recognizing that overt attempts at empathy may be painful or threatening to the patient, who is now aware that he does not have the same capacity.

It is rare for an antisocial patient to get to an uncovering or really insight-oriented phase of therapy. But if the patient has developed the degree of self-control and tolerance for distress that this work requires, he or she may be able to rework some traumas and deficits in learning that lead to a more durable result and an internalized set of rules. However, the changes may not be based on true identification, guilt, or shame.

Individual Psychotherapy

Insight therapy does not work with Antisocial Personality Disorder. Until recently, no controlled studies showed that there was any effective therapy for it. More recent studies now show some improvement may be possible with certain types of therapy. But you still can't hope to achieve full remission. Therefore, it is important not to try to bite off more than you can chew. Don't promise the patient more results than can be delivered at our current state of knowledge. You may want to target specific symptoms for a brief course of therapy. And no therapy may often be the best therapy.

Unlike conventional psychotherapy, therapy with a patient with ASPD should not be based on the relationship with the therapist. Often, the transference role the therapist plays is obvious. Transference may be very palpable. However, when recognized, the therapist should keep interpretations of transference to himself or herself. They are rarely useful to the patient. The material the patient presents about early life trauma and subsequent adventures may be fascinating from a dynamic viewpoint. Some had rotten relationships with their mother and act out their aggression in crimes toward women. Some were oedipal victors due to absent fathers, and they commit crimes without guilt, out of a sense of entitlement. Some carry out sibling conflicts in violent competitive struggles with peers. Unfortunately, however, such reconstructions of early life experiences are usually used as excuses for current antisocial behaviors, rather than as tools to promote change.

Therapy should be reality-based. The thinking process of a person with Antisocial Personality Disorder tends to be concrete, like that of a three-year-old child. Abstract notions like responsibility for his actions and for his life and empathy for how other people might feel about his behavior are difficult for him. Therapy should focus more on confrontation of his idealizing or omnipotent fantasies and angry acting-out behaviors rather than on interpretation of them. It should not encourage regression.

The life of a patient with an erratic, impulsive personality disorder is a mess because he doesn't have a normal amount of self-control. There is no "observing ego" function. Like a three-year-old, when he feels like doing something, he is consumed with the desire to do it. He can think of nothing else. He has mood swings, with irritability, violent rages, and abysmal, suicidal, depressive moods. When he is having a mood swing, he is totally caught up in it. He can't imagine or even remember ever feeling any other way. His behavior is totally mood dependent. He leaves thought and self-control behind until the mood passes. His likelihood of acting on these impulses is high when he is sober but greatly magnified when he is intoxicated. Therefore, addressing substance abuse is key.

Imagine how a preschool teacher would deal with a misbehaving three-year-old. Advise him about the right way and the wrong way to get what he wants. Help him see that some of the things he does for fun are dangerous. Help him devise ways in advance to control his recurring dangerous impulses. At the same time, offer empathic support, steadying and advising him. "You may be right; life may be unfair. But this keeps happening. It looks like you're stuck with it. And your own behavior seems to be making it worse. So what are you going to do to deal with it?" You may need to refer him to someone specifically trained to do therapy with this sort of patient.

One approach to individual psychotherapy is to educate him about his illness. Discuss the signs and symptoms of his disorder. The older individual who has been in trouble more than a few times usually knows that something is wrong with him but can't understand what it is. He often believes no one else could understand it either. Read the *DSM* criteria to him. It is a tremendous relief to him to find out that someone knows what the problem is and that it has a name. You may want to be cautious about using the term *antisocial*. It is pejorative in common parlance or means "unsociable." But tell him that he has a personality disorder, which means he isn't crazy.

Acknowledge with him that despite the fact he is not crazy, his life is still a mess. Tell him you would bet that when he feels like doing something, he just does it, without thinking through the consequences. He will think he *must* do it. He will usually agree with you at this point. Then you can tell him that another of his problems is unpredictable and uncontrollable mood swings. Ask him if he often experiences "seeing red" or partial amnesia during a rage attack. One favor we can do him is to remind him that feelings are only feelings and they will pass if given time, perhaps in a safe place like your treatment facility. Tell him that he should make no important, irreversible, or life-changing decisions until he calms down. Depending on his level of sophistication and interest, you may want to go on about the serotonin hypofunction theory of the impulsive personality disorders.

The patient with Antisocial Personality Disorder will initially try to use this information to evade responsibility for his acts. Make clear that having a personality disorder does not at all reduce legal responsibility. You can tell him that it may not be his fault that he doesn't have the usual amount of self-control. It is not a diabetic's fault that his blood sugar is hard to control. But the diabetic must learn how to watch his diet and exercise and take his medicine to get his sugar in better control if he wants to live very long or very well. Similarly, if our patient doesn't learn how to control himself, he will continue to have a distressing life, or be injured, or injure others. Then our society will exert control by putting him in jail or in a mental hospital.

We don't expect the diabetic to get his blood sugar under control alone. It is too complicated. He needs expert professional help from his dietitian, from nurses and doctors, and even from other diabetics. It is just as complicated to learn how to live without the normal amount of self-control as it is to learn to live without the normal amount of blood sugar control. Thus, we can't expect the patient with Antisocial Personality Disorder to learn how to control his moods and impulses alone. There is another slogan from Alcoholics Anonymous that applies here: "You alone can do it, but you can't do it alone."

In any case, the patient has to be the one to decide what the goals and target symptoms of therapy are going to be. If he is in your program because of legal, family, or other pressures, his initial goal will be to get this bother over with and get out of there. It may help to point this out to him in a sympathetic way. Your job is then to help him find a goal he can identify with and see a need for. This may or may not be the goal you or his family or the legal system had in mind. He may or may not want to stop drinking or fighting or stealing or beating his spouse. More likely he wants to stop the unpleasant or bored feelings and stop losing his freedom or to start having more fun. In an ideal world, you would help him get past the stage of blaming these unpleasant experiences on not having some adventure or sex or chemical to get high on—or on random fate, or on malice on the part of conventional society. Failing that, you will have to settle for getting him to work on ways to get along without too much suffering in this life, however unfair his life seems to have turned out to be.

Cognitive and Behavioral Approaches

Cognitive and behavioral approaches have become standard in the treatment of many personality disorders. They provide a here-and-now, nontransference-based approach to specific symptoms and problem behaviors. In antisocial patients, cognitive approaches have been used to help patients manage their anger, evaluate risks and benefits of behaviors, and develop awareness of how their behavior affects others. Behavioral approaches have been targeted at reducing unwanted behaviors by providing new patterns of reinforcement. Both cognitive and behavioral approaches can be used to develop and reinforce new patterns of behavior and new coping strategies. These approaches can be applied in individual, group, or family therapy.

Empathy Training

Empathy training involves teaching the patient how to understand how others feel and how his actions affect others. In most prisoners with Antisocial Personality Disorder, this kind of training reduces the likelihood of rearrest and return to prison.

However, patients with psychopathy, mentioned earlier, are a special case. Empathy training actually makes them worse. Their already higher rate of rearrest and return to prison increases further after this kind of therapy. Perhaps they use information about how other people feel inside to become better predators. The character Iago, in Shakespeare's *Othello* demonstrates this as he speaks of his commander:

> *The Moor is of a free and open nature,*
> *That thinks men honest that but seem to be so,*
> *And will as tenderly be led by the nose,*
> *As asses are.*

Positive Reinforcement

Punishment seldom stops a patient with Antisocial Personality Disorder from repeating his mistakes. Many a patient with Antisocial Personality Disorder has an inborn physiological inability to learn on a gut level from the bad consequences of his previous actions or from negative reinforcement. Some have called this an "inability to learn from punishment." In some situations, this inability to react with dread of possible or even predictable consequences of his behavior can be an asset. He often becomes a successful warrior, frontiersman, or adventurer. Famous soldiers, winners of the Congressional Medal of Honor, have ended up in jail or on skid row when the war was over. It is harder to find a niche for someone with these talents in more civilized society. Of course, he has a much higher mortality rate in combat and, in civilian life, from suicide, homicide, accidents, or drug abuse.

Although punishment often does not motivate the patient with Antisocial Personality Disorder to stop the bad behavior, positive reinforcement and reward for good behavior may help. So although he can't learn what *not* to do, he will learn what gets him what he wants. The reward must follow the good behavior immediately, however. Define good behavior very concretely, not in terms of basic principles. Also, make rewards very specific and concrete, not abstract or general. Despite remarkable shrewdness, he can't think abstractly. Rewards should occur within a day. "If you don't curse the staff today, you can go to the cafeteria for breakfast tomorrow." One day of not cursing the staff is something he can do. A week of it is too much to ask. Despite this, a string of seven single days of not cursing the staff, rewarded by seven meals in the cafeteria, could actually happen. Remember, though, he has not stopped cursing you because he thinks it is wrong or because he understands how you might be offended by his words. He has just learned that it gets him what he wants.

The Value of a "Short Leash"

The inpatient with Antisocial Personality Disorder tends to disrupt the ward milieu. He breaks the rules, defies authority, and suffers narcissistic injury at the faintest of slights. He preys on the other patients, intimidates peers and staff, smuggles drugs and other contraband into the ward, and becomes a ringleader of rebellion.

You can deal with this risk by telling the patient in advance that it is part of his disorder to act like that. In anticipation of this, you will keep him on a very short leash. For example, if there is any rumor that he is intimidating other patients for cigarettes, you will curtail his smoking privileges for twenty-four hours.

Tell him you will take the least threatening behavior very seriously. He should know that he may rapidly find himself restricted to the ward, on suicide or assault precautions, or in seclusion and restraints. Tell him that the least infraction of rules will be grounds for summary dismissal from the hospital. Tell him that you know that he has all the self-control of a three-year-old, and you will deal with him as such. You will try not to allow him to hurt himself or anyone else with his tantrums. Tell him that this is not because you despise him (and this should be the truth) but because it is part of his problem, and you have to be realistic.

This realism extends to calling the police and pressing charges if he breaks the law. Smuggling drugs, stealing from the hospital or his peers, communicating threats, or committing assaults probably are the most common infractions among inpatients. Tell him that if you charge him or if you find he has charges pending, your policy is to release him immediately to arresting officers. If he is suicidal or threatens suicide, tell the officers this so they can keep him on suicide watch in jail. This "natural consequences" approach is part of his therapy, too. He has a lesson or two to learn by going to jail. One of the lessons is that he certainly needs to get mental health help before he breaks the law, not after. Another important lesson is that the mental health system is not a shelter from the consequences of his acts. After he has served his time, he can come back to get the sort of therapy you offer.

You might also tell your outpatients in advance that illegal behavior is part of their problem but that you will deal with any new crime toward you through the legal system. Tell them that if you find yourself harmed or threatened, you plan to press charges.

Group Therapy

Until recently, no controlled studies proved that any therapy works with the antisocial personality. Now, however, studies are beginning to appear indicating that intensive therapeutic community treatment may be helpful. In one study, 65 percent of sixty-two subjects responded to the yearlong treatment; 55 percent of subjects stayed improved at follow-up eight months after discharge. Even before this, experts recommended group therapy for patients with Antisocial Personality Disorder for several reasons. The group situation dilutes the often intense positive and negative feelings of the patient toward the therapist. It decreases the risk of regression toward dependency on therapy. And it decreases the risk of intense rescuing or rejecting feelings by the therapist toward the patient.

As in Alcoholics Anonymous, group therapy may work because patients can see the character flaws in some other fellow just like themselves. They can see through the other fellow's rationalizing and evading responsibility because they do it so well themselves. And they can hear confrontation more easily from someone they identify with than they can from a staffer who "couldn't possibly understand" what they've been through or know where they are coming from. In England, there is a whole hospital devoted to the care of patients with Antisocial Personality Disorder. The current patients get to vote on who gets admitted to the program. The current patients have a vested interest in selecting new patients that they believe are motivated to change and thus can benefit from the program.

Family and Marital Therapy

There are at least four reasons why family or marital therapy may help the patient improve. First, when the family actually supports the patient's antisocial behavior, this needs to change. Second, the patient's relationship to his family members motivates him to get better more than does his relationship to you. Third, such therapy can teach the family members how to protect themselves from abuse or predation by the patient. This means assertiveness training. Advise them, as well, on how to get emergency advice from mental health professionals, how to petition for a mental health commitment, how to take out a restraining order, and when to call 911 for emergency police intervention. And last, confrontation by a patient's own family members about his misbehavior is more telling than confrontation by you. He can dismiss the latter as applying only to his relationship with you.

Other Psychosocial Interventions

Case management may be beyond the scope of many therapists' practices. However, failed communication among the different systems that antisocial characters become involved in may result in a lower chance of any treatment being helpful. For example, when patients bounce back and forth between caregivers without communication between them, the extent of antisocial personality problems may not be immediately evident to the new therapist or caseworker. When communication from the legal system to the therapy system doesn't happen, important diagnostic information may not be available. This can lead to unrealistic expectations and frustration in therapy and, at worst, to victimization of the unknowing therapist. Sometimes it is appropriate for therapists to make recommendations for interventions to other systems, like the criminal justice system or the department of social services. The following case study illustrates the nature of the problems that can arise from failure of communication (and cooperation) among systems to determine the best disposition for a patient.

CINDY

Cindy was a seventeen-year-old high school student who was hospitalized on the inpatient psych unit for the fifth time because she had exhibited destructive behavior in her foster home and gotten herself suspended from school for fighting. She was hostile and volatile when admitted, but calmed down within twenty-four hours of admission and stated that her behavior was related to wanting to move out of the foster home.

Her history was one of repeated foster home placement after she was removed from her family of origin at age six. At that time, her family of six siblings were all removed from the home because of the discovery of sexual and physical abuse by the father and alcohol abuse by the mother. For a time, she lived in common foster homes with an older sister. But when they began to plot schemes to vandalize their foster home in an attempt to be placed back with their own family, they were split up. Cindy had had at least thirty foster home placements since that time. She predictably got out of each placement by committing an act of vandalism or in some way terrorizing the foster parents until they requested that she be moved.

She'd had one six-month placement in a very structured corrective school for girls. She'd thrived in that environment. However, her behavior improved so dramatically that she was "mainstreamed" and put back in public school. Her behavior again deteriorated rapidly. Cindy stated that her one true goal was to "get back with my momma when I'm eighteen, or sooner if they'll let me." She described her antisocial behaviors as a deliberate attempt to send a message to the system that foster home placement wasn't working and that she wouldn't let it work. However, she was able to acknowledge that despite her tough, aggressive exterior, she was really distressed about being separated from her family and felt especially vulnerable to abuse by men. She also acknowledged that she had "a hot temper" and had learned to enjoy using it to intimidate others to get her way. She viewed psychiatric hospitalization as a convenient way to "get the system to do what I want."

She was discharged from the hospital after a few days to her previous foster home, which was willing to take her back. However, she appeared in the emergency room again several days later under petition for commitment because of assaultive behavior toward her foster parents. She had had to "up the ante" to get what she wanted. Thus, in Cindy's case, there was a lack of communication between the therapy system and the legal system regarding what was being played out and the options for dealing with it.

Medications

There is no medication that treats Antisocial Personality Disorder per se, but some specific symptoms may improve with medication. Any co-morbid Axis I disorder needing medication should get it. You will have to weigh constantly the risk that the patient will use the medication abusively or as an overdose. If he pleads for more because he lost it, or it was stolen, or he spilled it in the toilet, or because he is taking a trip and needs an extra supply, be alert. The odds are that he is actually abusing it, selling it, or hoarding it for an overdose.

First of all, what drugs should not be used? He will likely have impressive amounts of anxiety and will have had relief from abusable medications in the past. So he will put a lot of pressure on you to get him some more. It is important to emphasize that controlled medications like benzodiazepines (Valium and so on) can almost never be used in these patients. If a drug can be abused, these patients will abuse it. Every so often, we start to believe that one of those benzodiazepines is not abusable and can be used with this group of patients. A few years ago it was Xanax. More recently it is Klonopin. We keep learning the hard way. If your patient is getting these drugs, you can assume that he is abusing them or selling them on the street to other abusers.

SUSAN

Susan was a thirty-year-old woman in treatment for panic disorder and depression with a novice therapist. She had a history of impulse-control problems such as shoplifting and binge eating. She had been involved in check forgery, welfare fraud, and stealing from friends. She was secretly unfaithful to her boyfriend on many occasions but continued to live with him because he paid the rent. She described in detail all the symptoms of panic attacks and was prescribed an antidepressant and small doses of Klonopin (a high-potency benzo-diazepine). There was much confusion about lost and stolen prescriptions, and the therapist soon became aware that the patient was using more Klonopin than intended. Limits were set: the prescriptions had to be in writing, and if lost, they could not be replaced or refilled.

This worked for several months. Then the patient described a sudden increase in symptoms and demanded a higher Klonopin dose, refusing the therapist's suggestion that they change her anti-depressant dose instead. When the therapist refused and questioned the need for a sudden increase in Klonopin, the patient divulged that she had been selling the Klonopin instead of taking it and needed more because she was "short on cash." She was livid that the therapist would not continue prescribing!

Some personality disorder patients get a disinhibiting effect from benzodiazepines and become "paradoxically" more agitated when medicated with them. If your patient has a history of being much more violent when drinking or using other depressant drugs, anticipate that he will also become more violent on benzodiazepines. Antidepressant medications are just as effective for anxiety disorders but harder to abuse. The more sedating antidepressants, such as doxepine (Sinequan), however, are frequently abused by patients with Antisocial Personality Disorder. Doxepine has a reputation among prisoners for turning "hard time" into "easy time."

Second, treat any associated Axis I disease that the patient with Antisocial Personality Disorder often has. He has a 30 percent chance of getting Major Depression sometime in his life, usually after age thirty. If you diagnose this, consider treatment with antidepressant medications. Lithium, Tegretol, or Depakote will be indicated if there is co-morbid Bipolar Affective Disorder. A fair number of these patients develop persistent psychotic symptoms, perhaps from persistent and severe drug abuse. Consider antipsychotic medications for them. Attention Deficit/Hyperactivity Disorder is common, too. Certain antidepressants work for this and are less prone to abuse than the stimulants usually prescribed.

Mood Swings and Impulsiveness. Reports are beginning to appear in the literature indicating that very high doses of medicines like fluoxetine (Prozac) can reduce the frequency and severity of mood swings and outbursts of anger, aggression, and reckless impulsiveness in patients with Antisocial Personality Disorder. The younger patient is likely to feel no need for any such medication if he sees his anger as an appropriate response to not getting his way. The older patient has had repeated rude awakenings to the fact that this strategy does not work. He may desire to reduce his tendency to explode. In addition, if the patient has pedophilia or some other undesired compulsive behavior, these medications may be helpful.

FANNY

Fanny, a twenty-year-old college student saw us at her family's behest. They alleged that she had assaulted her mother, threatening her with a knife to get money. She told us that she enjoyed spending money and that if her mother would not freely subsidize this, she felt entitled to obtain money by any means necessary. The patient also claimed that her family lied about or exaggerated her misbehavior. She had also stolen her mother's checkbook and forged thousands of dollars in drafts. She had made inquiries at a finance company about mortgaging her mother's house to get spending money.

Restlessness in school had been a problem since kindergarten. From her early teens, she had lied, stolen, been truant, and been unable to accept behavioral limits imposed by adults. She extorted thousands of dollars from her mother using the ruse that she needed the money to pay off drug dealers who threatened to kill her for nonpayment. She feigned pregnancy to extort money from a casual boyfriend and his family. Later she offered a couple thousand dollars to another casual boyfriend to use as he wished. She was surprised when she was raped by a stranger after she spent the night drinking with him in his motel room. She failed to appear in court for any of her eight traffic violations.

She had had a number of psychiatric hospitalizations since age fifteen, usually because of suicide attempts and suicidal ideas. A trial of psychotherapy was abandoned after several months because she would not cooperate, even walking out of sessions. A trial of the antidepressant drug bupropion was not helpful.

Her family history is pertinent in that her largely absent alcoholic father did not maintain regular employment or meet financial obligations.

On our evaluation, Fanny had no clinical evidence of a psychotic, mood, or dementing disorder. Our clinical impression was Antisocial Personality Disorder. We confirmed this with psychological testing and the Structured Clinical Interview for *DSM-III-R* for Personality Disorders.

The patient was initially remarkably open and reflective in individual psychotherapy. She began to admit that she had a problem with impulse control and a bad temper. The therapist noted that the patient's character deficits were clearly disproportionately large compared to the minimal psychic trauma she had suffered in her essentially normal childhood. A family session ended early when she became enraged because her mother refused to take her home at once. She stormed out of the room, shouting and cursing her mother, slamming the door. After several sessions, she appeared to become depressed and refused several psychotherapy sessions.

She began a course of high-dose fluoxetine (Prozac). Three weeks later, her family began to describe her as helpful around home and with others. When offered a choice about continuing the medication at four weeks, she elected to continue it, saying that she believed it was helpful. She said she felt more comfortable being alone and had less urge to flee her current difficulties. She was less irritable and more able to tolerate minor irritations. She felt less anxious and (for the first time since starting school) less restless. She could concentrate better and no longer felt depressed. She now rated her mood swings as much less severe. She no longer wanted to kill her mother.

Aggression and Irritability. Antipsychotic drugs like chlorpromazine (Thorazine) and haloperidol (Haldol) can be helpful for the specific symptoms of aggression and irritability. They have been used to control aggression since they first became available. Recent studies confirm that the dose for aggression is higher than that for psychosis. In addition to this, John Gunderson has pointed out that these neuroleptics are just as effective as tricyclic antidepressants for depression in patients with personality disorder.

Here are two stories of men helped by antipsychotic medications:

JOE

Joe, forty years old, was depressed because his wife had just left him. He had long been angry and irritable. When drunk, he would assault her and anyone else nearby. He came to therapy saying he was tired of fighting, tired of getting hurt. As an afterthought, he said he was tired of hurting other people, too. He came for care, wanting help in getting sober and with his depression. After detoxification from alcohol, we discussed using tricyclic antidepressants, but he said he wanted to take chlorpromazine. He had taken it before and had liked its effect. We discussed the risks of possibly irreversible tardive dyskinesia. He accepted the risks, and we hesitantly started at a low dose. He kept asking us to increase the dose. After twelve weeks, he was finally satisfied with the effect of 2,000 mg per day. He said that at this dose his depression had resolved, and he no longer felt like punching out anyone who made eye contact with him. He had a stiff shuffling gait and hunched shoulders, but this didn't interfere with his work much, and it didn't bother him. He said that if he could stay sober and calm like this for six months, perhaps his wife would take him back.

He came back a few weeks after changing to a new doctor. His new doctor was horrified that a person without psychotic symptoms was on 2,000 mg a day of chlorpromazine and refused to refill his prescription. He had gotten depressed and violent again.

MAC

Mac was wild in his youth, fighting, challenging teachers, bullying smaller children, torturing and killing puppies and kittens. As a young adult, he never kept a job and depended on handouts from his parents to support him and his cocaine habit. If their help was slow in coming, he would show up at the family store and threaten to kill them or create enough of a commotion to drive customers away. His family was at the end of their rope. He was still in his early twenties and couldn't yet see that he or his behavior was in any way responsible for his troubles. He had fifteen brief hospitalizations in less than a year, precipitated by suicidal or homicidal threats. He seemed unable to benefit from the best efforts of his treatment team to help him. After several of these hospitalizations, he didn't improve, and he concluded that his team was deliberately trying to deprive him of help and just trying to get rid of him. So each subsequent time he came in, he would threaten to kill his caregivers. He said he hoped that this would get him a new team that would finally understand him and know how to fix him.

When he had needed seclusion and restraint in the hospital, he had received haloperidol a few times to calm his explosive episodes, and he liked it. He said it was effective in calming him down and also made him feel less depressed. We discussed the risks (extrapyramidal symptoms and tardive dyskinesia) and benefits. He accepted these risks as acceptable in light of the life-threatening symptoms they might help relieve. He was titrated to 20 mg (the equivalent of 2,000 mg of chlorpromazine) per day. He then stayed out of the hospital for six weeks, a new record for him.

Tegretol, Inderal, Lithium.   Some patients respond to these medications with a decrease in frequency and severity of irritable, angry outbursts.

TREATMENT RISKS

The treatment of Antisocial Personality Disorder can be risky for both patient and therapist. The wrong therapy can be harmful. The patient can become a casualty of psychotherapy. He is prone to overdose on psychotherapy as well as on the psychiatric medications we give him. This is especially true in individual therapy. He is likely to have intense positive or negative feelings toward his therapist. He will have no insight that these feelings are not appropriate to a therapy situation or are not reciprocated. He will tend to act on these feelings and use them to excuse his misbehavior. There is a high risk of regression, with him becoming infantile or dependent on you.

Even worse is the risk of acting out barely contained socially unacceptable wishes and fantasies in therapy. This may lead to "stalking" the therapist. Therefore, therapy should be reality-based, as described earlier, rather than based on uncovering fantasy material or on the relationship with the therapist.

Countertransference

Therapists treating this population need to be very aware of their own reactions and motivations for being involved in this work. These patients, like no others, will challenge your view of your worth as a therapist. They will often provoke a mixture of strong negative feelings that can interfere with your being able to help them. Threatening behavior or sexual provocation may cause you to feel fearful and angry and, in the long run, to have a hateful, punitive, or vengeful attitude toward the patient. Being punitive will lead to the patient's flight from therapy.

Being manipulated or duped by the patient can evoke feelings of humiliation and retaliatory anger in you. You (and the patient) may become uncertain of your ability to provide treatment. These patients may delight in your being shocked, tricked, and defeated, so be prepared for blows to your sense of effectiveness.

It is useful to be able to admit "you got me that time." Acknowledge the patient's savvy or cunning, as well as the fact that he still feels the childish need to use such behaviors. It is also important to be able to concede defeat and stop treating the patient if you get involved in continuous control struggles or sense that the patient is just using you for some nontherapeutic purpose. There is no room for either punitive or rescuing attitudes in treating these patients. They will retaliate against your punishment and make you the "bad guy." And they will use your rescuing to suit their own purposes.

It is easy to be taken in by a charming psychopath, to be too gullible and eager to rescue him. On the other hand, it is easy to dislike people who do the things these patients do and to become too cynical, suspicious, and bitter. It is a good idea to deal with Antisocial Personality Disorder in a matter-of-fact way, much as we would deal with a misbehaving child.

You may find it useful to look on the patient with Antisocial Personality Disorder as a potential "late-bloomer." He may achieve his maturity and ability to control impulses much later than the rest of us do. The most intelligent or talented patient with the latest onset of conduct disorder and the least severe course improves the most and the soonest. You may be encouraged to hang in there when you believe that the patient may "grow out" of his personality disorder in middle age, if he can keep from destroying his life before then. Encourage your patients with this possibility as well, for some are able to find hope for their future in this.

One of the best ways to deal with your own difficult feelings in response to these patients is to separate your feelings about their bad behavior from your feelings about them as persons. There is good evidence from the study of risk factors for this disorder that tells us that these people don't just choose to act badly because they want to. Some inherit predispositions to impulsive, aggressive behavior from their relatives. These relatives and their neighbors model bad behavior for them and give no consistent discipline. It's helpful to think of them as doing the best they can to get by in life with what they have been able to learn so far. Other people do usually dislike their behavior, so these people really do live in a hostile, punitive world where love, trust, and attachment are not available. So why should they suddenly trust you or believe you want to help them? They have usually learned to get what they need by any available means and then to "cut their losses" and flee. Don't be gullible or condone bad behavior. But growth is possible if the patient can believe that life could be better and that he can have something to do with it.

Here is a story about a patient with Antisocial Personality Disorder who got better:

FRED

Fred was about fifty and built like one of those old fat-cat Tammany Hall cartoon figures, with big jowls, a big jaw, and a protuberant abdomen. He looked like he was comfortable throwing his weight around. He was at ease striking up a conversation with a stranger. He was president of his own successful small service company. But life had not always been so good. When he was younger, he was always getting in some kind of trouble, usually involving violence. With time and the help of therapy, he had grown out of that. But now he had a big, burly, nearly grown, intimidating-looking son with a short temper. Because he saw his younger self in his son, Fred put extra effort into teaching him how to divert his angry energies.

We first met his menacing-looking son when he came back after a hard run in the woods, heaving and sweating but over his tantrum. They attended a conservative church together that had strict behavioral expectations of its members, including forbidding the use of drugs or alcohol. Fred attributed a lot of his own and his son's ability to control themselves to this external structuring of their behavior.

But until the patient with Antisocial Personality Disorder gets better, we have to treat him as though he were a three-year-old. Initially we can't trust him with any adult responsibilities. Like a child, he has to prove that he can handle responsibility before he gets any. Throughout history, society has been protecting itself from these out-of-control fellows by stoning them, exiling them, or putting them in jail. If he breaks the law, the rest of society must protect itself. If he comes to us for help before he has broken the law, we might try to provide him another opportunity to learn how to accommodate society. We can still try to help him after he has broken the law if we happen to work in a correctional institution.

Therapy for the Therapist

Marsha Linehan has pointed out that therapists who treat patients with Borderline Personality Disorder need consultation or therapy for themselves. The same is true for those who care for patients with Antisocial Personality Disorder. The patient with Antisocial Personality Disorder is just as demanding. He is never satisfied with our best efforts. It is never his responsibility if things don't go well with him; it is ours. There is usually just enough of a grain of truth in his accusations to sink a hook into our sense of responsibility and make us feel guilty or inadequate. And we may even get posttraumatic stress symptoms just from listening to the horrible stories from his life. He will fail to pay our fees. If the insurance company pays him for our services, he will stick it in his own pocket. He may threaten suicide. But he is more likely to threaten us and our loved ones. We may start out with unrealistic hopes of rescuing him. After sad experience, we may have conscious or unconscious desires to punish him.

For all these reasons, it is vital to have someone with whom to discuss the case and our feelings and reactions to the case. If we are in a treatment-team setting, our fellow team members are invaluable for this. But the whole team may get caught up in the same crisis together. So having a person or a therapy group outside the case to talk to about our reactions and feelings is sometimes very helpful. This will keep you from making mistakes with the case based on those feelings. It will help you to stay happy with your work. If you are not working in a team setting, it may be a good idea to get an adjunctive co-therapist in on the case.

With the very worst cases you will have to gang up on the patient and get even more help. Outside prison, one patient can require the coordinated services of inpatient and outpatient teams of psychologists, psychiatrists, social workers, case managers, substance abuse specialists, activity therapists, crisis workers, and family therapists all working together to devise ingenious and shrewd solutions to seemingly unmanageable problems. They must figure out how to coordinate needed services without being pitted against each other by the patient's machinations. Still, when you are feeling really frustrated and helpless, it is heartening to see how many other good people are having difficulty with the patient, too.

ISSUES IN MANAGED CARE

Third-party payers want to keep their costs low. One way to do this is to deny care. Another way is for them to try to ensure that the care they are paying for is effective. We have to be accountable to the people who are footing the bill. You should be hearing—from others as well as from the patient—of change, of improvement in his outside life. Is he going to work more, fighting less? Is he spending money more responsibly? Is he spending more time with his wife and children? Because therapy for Antisocial Personality Disorder is frequently ineffective, these reports are crucial.

Accountability

Many patients with Antisocial Personality Disorder cannot be motivated to change, and others will not be able to change. In the former case, you should stop the therapy. In the latter case, you should consider consultation with experts in other types of therapy before you stop.

Most treatment should be done outside the hospital, in other institutional settings or the outpatient arena. Keeping hospital stays short is an obvious cost control measure. When a patient is acute and dangerous, a four- or five-day hospital stay is usually about right. The first one to three days are needed for detoxification or for the rage to subside. He needs another two days of perceiving himself locked up against his will in the loony bin in order to cool his heels, to receive education about the nature of his illness, and to ponder what it was that got him in there. The hope is that he will reconsider the notion that it was, as always, someone else's fault. But don't keep him for a week. That's when he starts to get nice and comfortable and institutionalized.

Rarely, detoxification or mood stabilization may take longer. Or a longer stay may be merited because the patient is having a dangerous episode of an Axis I disease or is having many crises close together. We then have to stay accountable to the patient, to ourselves as professional caregivers, and to society as a whole. This includes accountability to potential innocent victims and to general public safety. Even the third-party payer who would rather deny benefits doesn't want blood on its hands because it pressured for the early release of someone who was still acute and dangerous.

Cost Control

In an era when resources for mental health treatment are becoming more limited and measurable outcomes are used to justify therapy, it is becoming more and more difficult to justify spending the resources to engage this difficult population of patients in therapy. Most therapy will probably be directed at behaviors that these patients exhibit that are seen to be costly, whether to the health care system (repeated admissions, accidents, substance abuse) or the general social system (violent behavior, larceny) rather than at developing the patient's understanding of his antisocial character or his quality of life. Therapists and clinics may not be able to afford to treat patients with such poor prognosis, and capitated systems may try to shunt people with these problems into the justice system rather than identify them as patients. (Of course, the justice system is also overworked and may try to shunt their cases to us.) Therapists may find themselves in a role conflict, seeing themselves as both advocates for this population and as stewards of limited resources. There are no easy answers to resolving this conflict, but it seems obvious that since empathy plays a role in advocacy and this type of patient does not often invite empathy, this population is at risk of being neglected for study and treatment. Prison settings, where modification of behavior has obvious and immediate benefit for the institution, may become the only setting in which treatment can occur, and treatment programs there may grow.

Ethical and Legal Issues

Except when they are threatening or at risk for dangerous acts or when you are doing a court-ordered evaluation, patients with Antisocial Personality Disorder are as entitled to patient confidentiality as anyone. However, court decisions and laws have identified some cases where duty to society transcends patient confidentiality. You should consider informing the patient at the start about the limits of confidentiality. Then you won't surprise him when you say, "You know, I am required to report certain things like this if I become aware of them."

One such court decision led to the famous Tarasoff doctrine. It imposes a duty to prevent harm to an identifiable target of foreseeable violence. If the patient is acutely dangerous and there are no adequate outpatient options, you can dispatch this duty by referring him for a brief hospitalization until the mood passes. If the danger is not current but is recurring and could foreseeably happen in a future crisis, you should warn the party at risk as well as the police. The patient who wants to stay out of trouble will agree to this or will help you find a better way to obviate danger.

Many jurisdictions have defined other situations where you must breach confidentiality. Health care providers may be required to report child abuse or elder abuse when they become aware of it. Check with your local authorities.

This chapter has emphasized strategies and techniques for interviewing, diagnosing, and treating people with Antisocial Personality Disorder. In conclusion, we want to emphasize again some of the most important points to keep in mind in dealing with this difficult population. First, keep in mind that this personality disorder may be part of a patient's problem when you detect substance abuse, a history of trouble with the law, or an inability to hold a job or stay in relationships. Pay attention to your own sense of unease in interacting with the patient. Once you have made the diagnosis, look for factors that suggest treatability before making the decision to treat. The risk of suicide is very real, so treat mood and anxiety disorders, psychosis, and substance abuse when you see them.

If you treat, try to see the patient as doing the best he can do to survive. Avoid being judgmental, while circumspectly protecting yourself from the real risk of harm or of being "used." Set clear, consistent limits on what you will tolerate and what you will do. Be willing to stop therapy if it's not helping, if it is making the patient's behavior worse, or if you are ineffective because you feel threatened. Seek support, consultation, or therapy for yourself when needed.

Set realistic expectations for therapy, focusing on Axis I and specific behavioral changes, and keep the therapy reality-based. Try to maintain an attitude of cautious optimism, recognizing that many of these individuals cannot yet be treated effectively but that time is on your side, for with time, many will improve significantly. We hope that continued research and clinical trials will enable us to predict more reliably who can benefit from treatment and what treatments help the most.

NOTES

P. 123, *criteria used to define the disorder:* Hare, R. D., Hart, S. D., & Harpur, T. J. (1991). Psychopathy and the *DSM-IV* criteria for antisocial personality disorder. *Journal of Abnormal Psychology, 100*(3), 391–398.

P. 125, *In the current United States population:* Robins, L. N., Helzer, J. E., Weissman, M. M., Orvaschel, H., Gruenberg, E., Burke, J. D., Jr., & Regier, D. A. (1984). Lifetime prevalence of specific psychiatric disorders in three sites. *Archives of General Psychiatry, 41*(10), 949–958.

P. 125, *in Norwegian populations:* Torgersen, S. (1995). *Epidemiology of personality disorders in Norway.* Fourth International Conference of the International Society for the Study of the Personality Disorders, Dublin, Ireland.

P. 126, *replaced with depressive and somatic disorders:* Marmar C. R. (1984). The personality disorders. In H. H. Goldman (Ed.), *Review of general psychiatry* (pp. 422–425). Los Altos, CA: Lange Medical Publications.

P. 127, *only 10 to 30 percent of patients:* Hare, R. D. (1993). *Empathy training worsens psychopaths but helps other prisoners.* Third International Conference of the International Society for the Study of the Personality Disorders, Cambridge, MA.

P. 127, *by Cleckley in* The Mask of Sanity: Cleckley, H. (1964). *The mask of sanity* (4th ed.). St. Louis, MO: Mosby-Year Book.

P. 129, *Psychopathic Psychotic Disorder:* Srna, R. (1995). *Psychopathic Psychotic Disorder.* Fourth International Conference of the International Society for the Study of the Personality Disorders, Dublin, Ireland.

P. 134, *perhaps 30 percent of men with Major Depression:* Fava, M., Rosenbaum, J. F., McCarthy, M., Pava, J., Steingard, R., & Bless, E. (1991). Anger attacks in depressed outpatients and their response to fluoxetine. *Psychopharmacology Bulletin, 27*(3), 275–280.

P. 138, *Rage attacks are characteristic:* McElroy, S. L., Hudson, J. I., Pope, H. G., Jr., Keck, P. E., Jr., & Aizley, H. G. (1992). The *DSM-III-R* impulse control disorders not elsewhere classified: Clinical characteristics and relationship to other psychiatric disorders. *American Journal of Psychiatry, 149*(3), 318–327.

P. 149, *serotonin hypofunction theory:* Cloninger, C. R. (1987). A systematic method for clinical description and classification of personality variants. *Archives of General Psychiatry, 44*, 573–588.

P. 150, *Empathy training actually makes them worse:* Hare, R. D. (1993). *Empathy training worsens psychopaths but helps other prisoners.* Third International Conference of the International Society for the Study of the Personality Disorders, Cambridge, MA.

P. 151, *an inborn physiological inability to learn:* Hare, R. D., Frazelle, J., & Cox, D. N. (1978). Psychopathy and physiological responses to threat of an aversive stimulus. *Psychophysiology, 15*(2), 165–172.

P. 152, *Rewards should occur within a day:* Van Broek, G. J., Maier, G. J.,

McCormick, D. J., & Pollack, D. (1988). Today-tomorrow behavioral programming: Realistic reinforcement for repetitively aggressive inpatients. *American Journal of Continuing Education in Nursing, 19,* 1–11.

P. 153, *intensive therapeutic community treatment:* Dolan, B. M., Evans, C., & Wilson, J. (1992). Therapeutic community treatment for personality disordered adults: Changes in neurotic symptomatology on follow-up. *International Journal of Social Psychiatry, 38*(4), 243–250.

P. 154, *current patients get to vote:* Norton, K., & Dolan, B. (1995). Acting out and the institutional response. *Journal of Forensic Psychiatry, 6,* 317–332.

P. 158, *become "paradoxically" more agitated:* Gardner, D. L., & Cowdry, R. W. (1985). Alprazolam-induced dyscontrol in borderline personality disorder. *American Journal of Psychiatry, 142*(1), 98–100.

P. 158, *(Prozac) can reduce the frequency:* Coccaro, E. F., Astill, J. L., Herbert, J. L., & Schut, A. G. (1990). Fluoxetine treatment of impulsive aggression in *DSM-III-R* personality disorder patients [letter]. *Journal of Clinical Psychopharmacology, 10*(5), 373–375.

P. 159, *pedophilia or some other undesired compulsive behavior:* Kafka, M. P., & Prentky, R. (1992). Fluoxetine treatment of nonparaphilic sexual addictions and paraphilias in men. *Journal of Clinical Psychiatry, 53*(10), 351–358.

P. 160, *used to control aggression:* Extein, I. (1980). Psychopharmacology in psychiatric emergencies. *International Journal of Psychiatry in Medicine, 10*(3), 189–204.

P. 160, *the dose for aggression is higher:* McEvoy, J. P., Hogarty, G. E., & Steingard, S. (1991). Optimal dose of neuroleptic in acute schizophrenia: A controlled study of the neuroleptic threshold and higher haloperidol dose. *Archives of General Psychiatry, 48*(8), 739–745.

P. 160, *neuroleptics are just as effective:* Gunderson, J. G. (1986). Pharmacotherapy for patients with Borderline Personality Disorder. *Archives of General Psychiatry, 43*(7), 698–700.

P. 166, *need consultation or therapy for themselves:* Linehan, M. (1993). *Cognitive behavioral treatment of borderline personality disorder.* New York: Guilford Press.

7

COUNTERTRANSFERENCE AND THE DIFFICULT PERSONALITY-DISORDERED PATIENT

Howard E. Book

What is so difficult about the difficult personality-disordered patient? Usually, the difficulty has little to do with making the diagnoses or knowing the correct dosage of medication. The difficulty with these patients usually has to do with the relationship they form with us and, in particular, the kinds of emotions they stir up in us. Nessie, whom I had been seeing in psychotherapy, demonstrates many of the characteristics that we label "difficult." In this chapter I will describe a series of escalating interactions with Nessie, and then look at what I ultimately came to understand about her difficulties and about my difficulty in treating her.

Throughout this chapter I refer to the therapist as male and the patient as female. I would like to emphasize that I am doing this for purposes of clarity only, rather than being under the sway of a gender-bias countertransference response!

NESSIE

"I'm sorry I'm late," I apologized as I greeted Nessie in the waiting area.

"It's only a few minutes," she replied soulfully. "And I guess it's hard to be concerned with someone who is such a loser," she went on, absently stroking the scars that covered her left arm from wrist to elbow.

"No, that's not so. I *am* concerned. I do care. Look—I even gave you my home phone number for emergencies," I reassured her, all the while thinking to myself, "Jesus, no wonder I dread seeing her. She seems to be getting worse no matter what I do. Why is she so oblivious to my attempts to help her and to the concern I feel?"

Nessie is an unemployed waiflike twenty-two-year-old single woman whom I started treating in weekly outpatient psychotherapy five months ago. She was referred to the mental health clinic after taking an overdose of one hundred aspirin subsequent to a breakup with her boyfriend, Ralph.

In the last month, because of her concern about feeling no better, I began to see her more frequently. She responded with more sad apologetic complaints that she was feeling worse and worse.

Nessie was an only child raised by a mother whom she described as "always being there for me. Through my whole life. She really cares. She is interested in my life and always wants to know what's going on. She is always giving me good advice. I should have listened more to her about how men can treat you."

As treatment progressed, though, I was beginning to think of her mother as overconcerned, controlling, and intrusive. She seemed to interfere with Nessie's attempts to be her own person and find her own voice.

Nessie had only scattered memories of her air force father who abandoned the family when she was thirteen. Though she recalled that he was "strong, certain, and guiding," to me it seemed that Nessie minimized her father's style of rigidity and his tendency to use physical punishment. I was a bit concerned by how unaware she seemed of the impact on her and her mother of her father's sudden departure for another woman.

MY RESPONSE

Initially, I felt sorry for this delicate, vulnerable young woman with a past history of parental intrusive control and abandonment. I was also concerned about the current difficulties precipitated by Ralph's dropping her. It occurred to me that the breakup with Ralph echoed her father's earlier abandonment of the family. She seemed so lonely, so yearning for help, and so victimized. Despite an adolescent history of delicate wrist slashing, I thought she would be a good candidate for psychotherapy. I thought that her eagerness for treatment, her optimism about our therapeutic relationship, and the lack of self-harm over the past eight years augured well.

In recent weeks, though, I found myself wondering what I was doing wrong and why she was becoming more despondent, more beseeching. At the start of therapy she had been effusively grateful that I was taking her seriously, but in the past six weeks I was mostly hearing, "You don't seem to understand how terrible I feel." I tried to reassure her that I cared and understood that she *was* suffering. However, I found myself perplexed about what was going on. Why did she continually accuse me of not understanding and not caring? I *did* care, I *was* listening. What proof did she need?

Recently she had said, "Sometimes I figure if you really cared, you would hold me when I really get upset during the sessions." I had informed her that I couldn't offer her that kind of help; our job was to talk and try to understand more about why she felt so hopeless. But her request made me uncomfortable.

A few times, I found myself wishing, "Maybe she needs a woman therapist." Or "Maybe if she moved back to Minneapolis her troubles would be solved." Certainly, mine would. Invariably I would end up feeling guilty for these thoughts. On one occasion, to my horror, I even found myself thinking, "If she killed herself, I'd be rid of her." At other times, I had the fleeting thought, "Maybe if I *did* cuddle her she'd understand that I really do care."

Invariably, I'd end up feeling guilty and loathsome for harboring such "bad" thoughts. Most of the time, I just wondered why she was such a difficult patient.

What Is a "Difficult" Patient?

In discussions with other mental health professionals, I've been struck by how frequently we use the term *difficult* in discussing the personality-disordered patient. And with these patients, what's "difficult" for one therapist is usually "difficult" for another. Most of us, for example, would find Nessie to some degree difficult. Her lack of responsiveness to treatment, her inability to appreciate my concern, her dismissing of any positive gains I attempt to point out to her, and her quiet demand that I do more all stirred up in me feelings of impotence, defensiveness, and frustration.

And that is the core of what characterizes the adjective *difficult* when applied to personality-disordered patients; they usually have two common and linked characteristics despite their differing diagnoses: their behavior and our response.

Think for a moment of those patients in your practice that you consider difficult. How do they make you feel?

Chances are that these patients probably stir up in you feelings of impotence, dread, frustration, hopelessness, helplessness, fury, and fantasies of getting rid of them—as well as fantasies that they might relocate or even commit suicide.

Or they may also stimulate opposite but equally problematic feelings of specialness: the belief that only you *really* understand this patient, the impulse to see the patient more often for longer periods of time, thoughts of holding the patient, or even wishes to have sex.

Most of these feelings are difficult for us to admit, let alone tolerate. Why? Because most of us chose this profession in order to relieve the suffering of patients who wrestle with substantial emotional turmoil and psychic pain. The idea of feeling hopeless, of hating our patients or wishing them dead, strikes at the very core of our professional self-image as helpers and healers. Similarly, the belief that we have a very special relationship—that only with us does the patient have a definite chance for cure, and related fantasies of holding, caressing, or even having sex with the patient—are tremendously conflictual and distressing.

Not surprisingly, we respond to these disquieting feelings with powerful affects of guilt, self-criticism, and worry, as well as by attempting to dismiss or hide these ideas and sensations, even from ourselves. However, even out of our awareness, these feelings still affect our responses to our patients and often cause us unwittingly to behave in antitherapeutic ways. As this chapter will illustrate, these unconscious countertransference responses often paradoxically re-create between us and our patient the very same noxious relationship that existed early on between her and her childhood caretakers. And it's this earlier noxious relationship that has played a crucial role in the development of those psychological difficulties and relationship problems with which she currently presents.

However, because our countertransference feelings usually remain out of our awareness, we respond to these simmering impulses, wishes, and fears by attempting to overlook them or sweep them aside, and instead we label the patient as difficult.

Whose "Difficulty" Is It: The Patient's or the Therapist's?

You may note how I tended to blame Nessie for "not getting better" and for "driving me crazy," how at times I nurtured a hidden wish that she kill herself while at other times I had embarrassing fantasies of holding her to prove I cared. In fact, I'd gone so far as to give her my home telephone number to prove that "I was really concerned" about her. Both these feelings alternated with another set of emotions about myself: I felt abused, mistreated, misunderstood, and helpless.

In response to these feelings about her "specialness" and "potential" and my view of her having suffered so much, I bent the rules. I began to see her more frequently; our once-a-week sessions became twice and then three times a week. I gave her my home phone number for emergencies—but ended up feeling taken advantage of and finally furious as she began to phone more, rather than less. At times, my fury caused me to have fantasies of wishing her dead, but immediately I would berate myself for harboring such awful thoughts about such an unfortunate waif.

It was only after being on the phone with her at 2:00 A.M. one Thursday and then forgetting our 3:15 P.M. Friday appointment that I finally recognized how my responses to Nessie were interfering with our therapeutic contract. And I began to wonder whether she was really "difficult" to treat or whether *I* was simply having difficulty treating her.

Late that Friday afternoon as I left the clinic, I stopped a colleague in the hall: "Harold, I've got to have another consultation with you about a patient. She's getting worse. And so am I."

"What seems to be the trouble?" Harold asked.

"Well, I'm finding myself becoming increasingly anxious about her. I notice I'm bending the rules a little bit in order to help her feel safe. But rather than her being reassured, her problems seem to escalate." I went on to describe the escalating difficulties with Nessie and my own mounting fears and sense of hopelessness.

After a while, Harold interrupted, "You know, it's not uncommon for therapists who treat these kinds of patients to start extending themselves more and more while at the same time feeling less and less confident about their ability as therapists. This happens even to fairly seasoned clinicians. But I think it would be quite helpful," he went on, "if we sat down and had a formal consultation about this patient. I think that you deserve a fair amount of time to discuss what's happening within you as well as between you and your patient. A rapid three-minute hallway consultation won't be all that fruitful, but I think our spending some time looking at what's going on will. From what you've told me, I don't think she is going to deteriorate rapidly over the next few days. Why don't we meet next Tuesday? And in the meantime, you might spend a little time thinking about why you seem to be having such a strong response to her."

We met four days later on Tuesday.

THE CONSULTATION

"So, how are you?" Harold began.

"Actually, I feel better—less worried about Nessie."

"Good, good. Why do you think that is?"

"Well, I've given it a fair amount of thought since we last met. It's interesting because she hasn't changed. But I think I have." I continued, "In fact, I figure that your not getting caught up in *my* panic over Nessie really helped. And I felt reassured by your offer to meet with me today when we could discuss her and—as I realized—my *feelings* about her."

"I'm glad that was reassuring," Harold noted. "Do you have any idea why it comforted you?"

"Yeah, I think so. First, that you took my worries seriously was reassuring. Second, I figure, looking back at it, that you and I could not have accomplished much in a brief discussion. I probably would have only ended up feeling more frustrated and confused. And I realized that that's probably how Nessie feels after her 2:00 A.M. phone calls."

"Ah!" exclaimed Harold. "Good point. You noticed a parallel in how Nessie is so hungry for you and how hungry you sounded for a 'quick hallway-fix consultation.'"

"Yes," I continued, "and something else too. You were interested in my difficulties, but you were also able to draw limits around what you could offer in a three-minute busy hallway. And I realize that I should have been doing that with Nessie when she called me outside our usual contracted psychotherapy sessions."

"Assuming you took time to assess the seriousness of the situation and didn't automatically tell her you'd see her at the next session."

"Yes."

What I became aware of was how Harold had functioned as a "container" for my anxiety. He didn't become worried, anxious, and contaminated by my emotional turmoil. And this is what I should have been doing with Nessie: I should have been able to tolerate and contain her anxiety and demands and, in doing so, detoxify, neutralize, or metabolize them so that both she and I could attempt to understand them and their roots in an unpressured manner.

It reminded me of a book I had read recently, *Supervision in the Helping Professions,* by Hawkins and Shohet, who state that the therapist's role is not just to help the patient understand her difficulties but also to allow her emotional disturbance to be experienced within the safer setting of the therapeutic relationship. Within this setting, these feelings can be reflected on and learned from. The therapist thus provides a container that holds, tames, metabolizes, and detoxifies feelings that would otherwise be too unsettling for the patient to tolerate.

Why was I unable to function in this way? Let's return to my consultation with Harold.

"You mentioned a few moments ago," Harold went on, "that we might spend this time talking about Nessie *and* your feelings about her. Tell me more about how your feelings might be playing a role in the difficulties you have treating her."

"Well," I said, "I think I am having countertransference difficulties that interfere with my clinical decision making."

"Tell me about it. But first, tell me what your understanding is of 'countertransference feelings.'"

"Classical" Countertransference Reactions

"Well," I began, "countertransference is a term that refers to *unconscious* feelings that I experience toward my patient because at an unconscious level she reminds me of a person from my past. And I misrespond to that patient—in this case, Nessie—with feelings, attitudes, behaviors, and concerns that are really meant for and directed to another earlier person from an earlier time."

"That's right," Harold replied. "Countertransference refers to dormant feelings, attitudes, behaviors, and concerns that were initially aimed at past significant adults from the therapist's childhood but that become revived, reactivated, and reexperienced, not as belonging to a distant time and different person but as occurring now, in the present, with the patient. What you have to keep in mind, though," Harold emphasized, "is that all these countertransference feelings occur *outside* of the therapist's awareness. And usually to such an extent that the therapist, unaware of how these countertransference feelings are fueling his behavior, rationalizes and makes excuses for this antitherapeutic behavior."

"I think that's exactly what's happening with Nessie and me," I commented. "In some way, she reminds me of a significant figure from my past and has stirred up behaviors and concerns of mine that were really not meant for her, but were a revival, a repetition of a reaction to a significant person from my childhood."

"Right," Harold said. "That definition of countertransference is known as the 'classical' definition. I want to hear more about it. But first, I should mention that there is another countertransference called the 'totalistic' countertransference, which we will talk about later. But for now, tell me about what you think was occurring in this classical countertransference reaction you had to Nessie."

"Well, once I settled down a bit, I wondered why I was reacting so worriedly to Nessie and why I was making exceptions for her like giving her my home phone number and tolerating her calling me at two in the morning. So I wondered whether in some ways she reminded me of anyone from my past.

"At first, I didn't think so," I went on. "I couldn't think of any woman she was similar to. But then I suddenly realized that countertransference feelings are not necessarily gender specific.

She could, in some way, remind me of a man. And bam!, my uncle Phil immediately came to mind."

I went on to outline to Harold how my father's younger and troubled brother frequently and frighteningly had interfered with our family life. Phil was unsuccessful, had significant alcohol problems, and frequently phoned our home pleading for my father's help. I recalled my father going out in the middle of the night to find Phil, how worried he became when he couldn't find him, and how my father's upset was so easily transmitted to me. And how I, too, would worry about Phil and the impact he was having on my father.

"At times when he stayed with us, Phil would also tell me his troubles. I was just a kid, but I'd feel badly. I tried to show him card tricks to cheer him up. I remember feeling doubly badly then because showing him how to do card tricks was against the magician's code."

"What happened with Phil?" Harold asked.

"One day he crossed the street against the red light. I guess he was drunk. A car hit him. He died.

"It's funny," I concluded, "but from time to time I am aware of these issues when I treat older male patients—particularly those with alcohol or drug problems. I've just never thought that these feelings could be called up by a young female patient."

Harold cleared his throat and looked at me over his glasses. "Countertransference is not gender specific. Women patients don't necessarily stir up feelings you may have had for your mother, nor do men patients evoke feelings you had for your father. What you describe is a perfect example of this. Nessie's neediness and helplessness seem to have reactivated those dormant feelings related to your ambivalent concerns about Uncle Phil—feelings related to a sense of obligation to help him, frustration and helplessness about your inability to do so, and hidden feelings of guilty irritation. These were feelings connected to your early experiences with Phil, but they rose up and became "attached," so to speak, to Nessie. And in experiencing them with Nessie, these issues and concerns interfered with your usual ability to maintain objectivity in the face of her difficulties. You responded to her as if you were still that eleven-year-old boy and she were your uncle Phil whom you were so desperately trying to save while simultaneously fighting off awareness of your mounting irritation at being so used."

Harold shifted slightly in his chair and continued, "And in responding this way, you lost your usual calm, concerned, and objective stance. Under the sway of these classical countertransference feelings, you felt pressure to save her, rather than attempting to understand the relationship between Ralph's leaving her and her impulsively taking an overdose. Similarly, you overlooked how this self-destructive behavior echoed her wrist slashing when her father abandoned the family.

"Your responses to her were powered by classical countertransference reaction reflecting your relationship with Phil, rather than being a clinically indicated intervention.

"Your giving her more and more also implied a promise of unending, always available support. But such promises will only fuel the difficult personality-disordered patient's hunger. The more you are influenced by your countertransference feelings to give, rather than to understand Nessie's pressured needs, the more you fuel her neediness. And it also frightens these patients that they are so powerful that you, the therapist, are too helpless or frightened to limit those demands."

"Are you saying you don't give extra sessions or hand out telephone numbers?"

"Only if either one is objectively and clinically indicated. Only when it's a reflection of the patient's status—such as in emergency or crisis situations. And not because of the therapist's countertransferential difficulties around a wish to be liked, or difficulty setting limits, or fear of the patient's aggression, and so on.

"As you might notice," Harold emphasized, "the classical countertransference response reflects what the *therapist* 'brings to the table.' It's part of his 'emotional baggage.' It is an unconscious reaction emanating *from within* the therapist."

The Need to Monitor Your Own Behavior

"How do you know when this kind of countertransference is occurring?" I asked.

"To spot any kind of countertransference—be it this classical kind or the totalistic kind, which we'll discuss in a moment—the therapist continually has to monitor his own behavior and feelings toward the patient."

"What do you mean?"

"Well, the therapist not only needs to listen to what the patient is saying but he should also be listening to what *he* is saying, thinking, or feeling. The therapist should continually be wondering, 'Am I saying and doing this because it is clinically indicated or because it has to do with what *I* feel, want, am curious about? Or because of my own needs not to feel disliked, helpless, guilty, or angry?'

"And if this is so, if the therapist seems to be responding because of his own needs, he should take the next step and ask himself, 'Who does this patient remind me of?' And if these feelings seem to arise over and over or make it impossible for the therapist to behave therapeutically, then the therapist should seek consultation, supervision, or even treatment himself in order to understand and resolve these ongoing and significant early conflicts."

"Totalistic" Countertransference Reactions

"You mentioned there is another kind of countertransference?" I inquired.

"Right," Harold stated. "It's called *totalistic* countertransference. Like the classical countertransference, the totalistic countertransference also consists of the same unconscious disquieting feelings, attitudes, and behaviors—feelings of rage toward the patient, fear of the patient, wishes to rescue the patient, desires to kill the patient, hopelessness over ever helping the patient, dread on hearing the patient's name, wishes to hold, fondle, and have intercourse with the patient. Since they are unconscious, these wishes operate beyond the therapist's awareness. Also, like the classical countertransference, these unconscious feelings can derail the therapist from practicing competent psychotherapy."

"Yeah, I understand that so far," I interrupted, "but how does the totalistic countertransference *differ* from the classical countertransference?"

"The difference," Harold explained, "is that the classical countertransference refers to what's already 'inside' the therapist. What he brings to the table from *his* past; his emotional baggage that is activated because the patient unconsciously reminds him of an important person from his past. Nessie, for example, with her 2:00 A.M. phone calls awakened all those dormant feelings you had about your uncle Phil with his frantic midnight appeals to your father.

"Now, the totalistic countertransference refers not to what's already inside the therapist but to what the patient *puts* inside the therapist."

"What do you mean by the patient 'putting something inside' the therapist?" I broke in.

"Well," Harold continued, removing his glasses, "patients evoke—or 'put inside' the therapist—certain feelings by virtue of the manner in which they tell their stories, the way they treat the therapist, and the attitude they bring into therapy. It's not so much their words—not so much the content—but rather the *manner*, the *way* they relate to the therapist that causes the therapist to experience certain feelings. It's not so much the 'words' as it is the 'music.' And generally speaking, the more personality disordered the patient, the more troublesome the feelings they evoke in the therapist.

"In addition, these feelings tend to occur regardless of the therapist's background. That is, the more personality disordered the patient, the more likely the therapist is to experience particular feelings—regardless of who the therapist is and what the therapist's own background is like. If you have ten different therapists from ten different backgrounds, who are all seeing the same difficult personality-disordered patient, it is quite likely that all ten therapists will experience many of the same kinds of feelings."

"You mean," I interrupted, "the totalistic countertransference response reflects the *patient's* problem—what the patient puts into the therapist—much more than any particular problem from the therapist's past."

"That's it!" Harold exclaimed. "That's the whole concept of the totalistic countertransference. Glen Gabbard, who has a great deal of experience treating difficult personality-disordered patients, has co-written a book, *Management of Countertransference with Borderline Patients.* He notes that these patients often rid themselves of tension by evacuating or 'dumping' their problematic feelings into the therapist."

A Joint Creation

"The point I'm making," Harold continued, "is that the *way* the difficult personality-disordered patient behaves in the presence of the therapist produces intense feelings within that therapist. However, because these feelings are often embarrassing, guilt inspiring, shameful, or otherwise troublesome, the therapist's automatic defense mechanisms keep them out of awareness. Still, even though they are unconscious, these countertransference feelings infiltrate and distort the mental health professional's competence."

"Could this be happening to me?" I asked.

"I think so," Harold replied. "You see, these two countertransference reactions, the classical countertransference and the totalistic countertransference, are not mutually exclusive. A therapist can experience both simultaneously. In fact, it's probably best to view countertransference as a joint creation consisting of both what the therapist brings from his past (classical countertransference) and what the patient 'puts' into him (totalistic countertransference)."

Harold went on, "You quickly and astutely pointed out your classical countertransference: how Nessie reminded you of your uncle Phil and reawakened already existing but dormant and unresolved feelings from your childhood relationship with him. However, I think there's more going on than just that classical countertransference response."

"Go on," I urged.

"I think that by her attitude and behavior toward you—that is, through the relationship she has attempted to forge with you— Nessie has put something of herself, part of herself *into* you. She disowns and projects into you troublesome aspects of herself. And by doing so, she attempts—unconsciously, of course—to force you to behave and feel a certain way toward her.

"What I'm getting at," Harold explained, "is that through her behavior to the therapist, the difficult personality-disordered patient unconsciously attempts to re-create in the here and now that early troublesome relationship she had with her caretakers. And it is from this early troubled relationship that most of her current relationship problems emerge.

"At times during therapy, the difficult personality-disordered patient unconsciously attempts to cause you to feel the very way *she* did in that earlier troubled relationship. At other times, this same patient attempts to make *you* feel and respond the way she experienced her *caretaker* as behaving to her in that earlier distressing relationship."

"Wait a second," I responded, "you mean there are times in therapy when Nessie attempts to make me feel as miserable as she was in that earlier pivotal relationship?"

"Yes. From what you've told me about Nessie's upbringing," remarked Harold, "I'm hypothesizing that she attempts to make you feel as overtly compliant but hiddenly furious as she was in relationship with her controlling and intrusive mother."

"And you're also saying that at other times she attempts to get me to treat her the same way she experienced her mother as treating her?"

"Yes," Harold agreed. "I'd guess that at other times she's also attempting to get you to behave in the same controlling, intrusive, and fretful manner her mother did."

"That's ridiculous! Why in the world would Nessie—or anyone—want to *re-create* with their therapist a distressing and unsatisfactory relationship? It seems to me she would want to forge a new, different, better, more rewarding relationship!"

"Oh," responded Harold, "Nessie wants to do that too. Actually, difficult character-disordered patients are attempting to do both. First, they unconsciously attempt to re-create that pivotal noxious relationship from their past. They do so by unconsciously attempting to put the therapist into the role *they* had with their caretaker—that of the mistreated child. And that's how Nessie makes you feel: beleaguered, mistreated, your good intentions unacknowledged. And in that situation, they tend to play out the role of their caretaker: demanding, intrusive—just as Nessie is to you with her 2:00 A.M. phone calls.

"At other times, they try to force the therapist to behave toward them in the unsatisfactory way they experienced their caretaker as being. And at the same time they enact the role of victimized child. For instance, from what you've said, I think you may be quite angry at Nessie because she isn't improving and because of her quiet complaints. And it is this anger that fueled your fantasies of her suiciding and provoked you to forget her 3:15 Friday appointment.

"Psychotherapy helps because it allows the patient an opportunity to re-create this pivotal distressing relationship in a forum where the therapist can then identify and help the patient to understand the roles she plays and the role the caretaker played, with the goal of resolving this legacy of a tormenting relationship the patient carries within her. This offers the patient the opportunity to understand and resolve these roles rather than enacting them with every significant person with whom she enters a relationship. As a result, a more nurturing, helpful, and supportive relationship can develop."

"I kind of see how this *is* happening between Nessie and me," I slowly replied, "but I still don't understand why she—or any other patient—would want to re-create an earlier noxious relationship in the present with their therapist."

"Good question."

Reasons Why Patients Re-create Noxious Relationships

"And it's an important one that puzzles most therapists," Harold went on. "If you can appreciate the answer, it may help you understand—rather than be puzzled by—Nessie's demands and your totalistic countertransference reactions.

"You are wondering why in the world Nessie—or any other character-disordered patient—would want to recreate with you, her therapist, the very crippling relationship from which her current difficulties emerge. Well, there are four central reasons why this happens. All these reasons are outside the patient's awareness."

Re-creation as a "Test."

"First," Harold stated, "on an unconscious level, Nessie is probably thinking, 'You say you're here to help and protect me? Well, I've heard it before. My parents were supposedly here to help and protect me too. But they didn't. And neither has anyone else who said he cared. So why should I believe you? What I am going to do is push you to see if you will fail me in the same ways my parents failed me. I will recreate the same scenario, push you to behave as they did, and see if you fail or come through for me. Only then will I know for sure whether it's safe to expose myself, to show you my concerns, to make myself vulnerable in your presence.'

"You see, generally speaking, patients will only allow unconscious and personal material to come into consciousness and will only begin to share these concerns after they have concluded it is safe to do so. Because the difficult personality-disordered patient often comes from a background where she felt misused and misunderstood, she is subtly and unconsciously primed to provoke the therapist in order to see if he is going to respond the way early caretakers did. Or whether the therapist is indeed as professional and trusting as he holds himself to be. Only when the therapist has 'passed' this test does the patient feel comfortable and trusting enough to discuss these hitherto unspeakable concerns."

Re-creation as Container. "At times," Harold went on, "patients 'put into' the therapist their own intolerable feelings and internal dramas because they don't have mature enough ego functions to contain and tame these raw affects. They put these raw emotions and struggles into the therapist for 'safekeeping.' Therapists who are aware of how they are being treated and aware of the feelings that are being deposited in them—such as rage and retaliation—can model for the patient a way of containing and taming these feelings. Only then can these feelings be looked at, understood, discussed, or resolved."

Re-creation as a Defense Against Abandonment. "There is another common reason why patients re-create troublesome relationships," Harold noted. "Nessie, for example, may be unconsciously attempting to re-create that noxious but same relationship because it is *familiar.* And the familiar and known—even when painful—are less frightening than the unfamiliar and unknown. Particularly because the unfamiliar and unknown carry with them threats of abandonment, and issues of abandonment are often central to the personality-disordered patient's difficulties."

Re-creation as Communication. Harold stopped for a moment, as if to emphasize the significance of what he was about to say.

"This last reason is perhaps the most important and common dynamic explaining why patients re-create troublesome relationships. It reflects the difficulty these patients have acknowledging, identifying, tolerating, putting into words, and sharing with the therapist internal experiences and forgotten memories.

"The primary manner that patients like Nessie have of communicating these difficult experiences and relationships is by unconsciously enacting them—re-creating them—with the therapist.

"The key dynamic is that Nessie unconsciously reenacts early crucial problematic relationships while wordlessly pushing the therapist to take on, unconsciously, an earlier role because *it is the only way she can communicate this early experience.* It is the only way because she, like other personality-disordered patients, doesn't have the capacity to identify and put into words these experiences. So she enacts them with the therapist and pushes the therapist to enact them too."

"What do you mean by unconsciously pushing the therapist too?" I was puzzled.

"That is the critical aspect," replied Harold. "At times, without realizing it, as I've suggested, Nessie plays out the role of victim with you, while simultaneously pushing you to behave as if you were her early abuser. Thus her complaints of not improving, and your cutting off the session before it is time to end.

"At other times, again outside her awareness, she plays out the role of abuser and causes you, without recognizing it, to feel and begin to behave like the victim. As I pointed out, she intrudes into your life at two in the morning and leaves you feeling helpless to fend her off and futile in your attempts to help her.

"And all these enactments occur invisibly—out of the awareness of the patient certainly but also out of the awareness of the therapist.

"It is a therapist's task to become aware of the role he is being forced into, the feelings evoked, the impulses experienced, and the temptations he experiences to behave in certain ways.

"Let me tell you about a patient whose behavior and attitude produced a dramatic totalistic countertransference response in me. And you'll see how this totalistic countertransference response had enormous communicative value.

"I was once asked to do a consultation on a complaining and physically preoccupied patient. I was, however, unprepared for the psychotic man standing in front of me in my waiting area. His eyes were darting, his shoulders hunched, he was pinching his arms and sobbing tearlessly. On occasion he would shout, 'No, no, not again, not again.'

"I must say I was not prepared for what I saw, and it made me quite nervous. In order to make myself feel better, I quickly began doing a formal assessment of his mental state. My patient behaved as if I were not present.

"Doing a mental status evaluation didn't help him at all, but it helped calm me. And as my nervousness receded, I was able to sit comfortably enough with this man and observe him *and my own feelings* in his presence. As I did, a slowly unfolding fantasy came into my consciousness in which I was pleasurably pinching him! As I tormented him in my fantasy, he would writhe with pain. Focusing on this fantasy, I realized that his twisting and anguish within my mind fit perfectly with his writhing movements in the chair across from me. Now, although I could see that this fantasy was partially born of my frustration and irritation about this mute patient, I was also intrigued by how closely his movements in my mind paralleled his actual behavior in the chair.

"I could not think of anyone he reminded me of, so I did not believe that I was experiencing a classical countertransference reaction.

"And—thinking more about how his movements in my mind paralleled his actual behavior in the chair—I began to wonder about the communicative value of this fantasy, this totalistic countertransference response. In other words, perhaps he was experiencing what I was fantasizing. Or more accurately, I thought that his terrible experience was evoking this fantasy in me.

"So, using the communicative value of my countertransference responses, I ultimately said something like 'From your behavior I have the idea that you feel connected to an evil force that torments you any time you begin to tell me what is happening.' He stopped rocking, sat up, and stated, 'That's right. It's been going on for four months now. They punish me terribly when I start to talk about it. It is a relief to realize that somebody is aware of what's going on.' He continued talking for a few more minutes before becoming quite psychotic again.

"I bring up this example because it highlights the importance of paying attention to one's own internal experiences in order to gain access to the inner world of a patient who is unable or unwilling to talk about his inner experiences. Communicating the understanding that emerged through my countertransference response briefly offset his regressive state and allowed him to feel more consolidated so that he was able to experience and explore affects that had previously been intolerable. In addition, this understanding that I communicated provided an essential ingredient in the formation of a therapeutic alliance."

The Importance of Paying Attention to Your Own Feelings

"It is essential for us therapists to recognize when we have these feelings and impulses toward the patient. Why? Because many of these feelings—fury, dread, the wish to be rid of, the wish to hold—are experienced by therapists as 'bad'; they seem shameful or guilt inspiring. Therapists often feel that 'these are not the kinds of feelings competent therapists should have.'"

"But isn't that so?" I asked.

"No," Harold replied. "As I pointed out earlier, competent therapists are allowed any kind of feeling toward their patients. What makes a therapist competent is his ability to recognize, tolerate, contain, and *understand* these feelings. And to do this in the context *of what he brings to the table from his past*, like you and your feelings about Phil. But also—as we're discussing now—in the context *of what the patient is putting into him:* feelings the patient is silently forcing him to experience and roles she is invisibly pressuring him to enact.

"As I was saying, it is the therapist's task not to act on these wishes but to recognize, tolerate, and contain them. And *then* attempt to understand these internal experiences, first in the context of his own past and then as potentially valuable information that the patient may be putting into him. Viewed this way, totalistic countertransference is *a form of communication by which the patient wordlessly informs the therapist of her early experiences with caretakers:* how she felt, as well as how she experienced others behaving toward her. All of this may be contained in the wishes and the impulses that the therapist experiences in his relationship with the difficult personality-disordered patient.

"Once the therapist is aware of this totalistic countertransference and its meaning, he can share this new knowledge with the patient in order to further her understanding of early experiences with caretakers and of the ways in which these experiences play a role in current relationship problems.

"The key concept is that all of us—but especially the difficult personality-disordered patient—carry around inside ourselves hidden memories of what we experienced in early contentious relationships with caretakers. In therapy these become stirred up, and to avoid remembering them, the patient dumps them into the therapist. So then it is the therapist, rather than the patient, who feels and is pressured to behave like the victimized child.

"And here is what is so often missed: difficult personality-disordered patients also carry around inside them hidden attitudes and behaviors *that their caretakers showed toward them.* They take in the very attitudes that they believe caused their problems, the attitudes and behaviors that they railed against in their caretakers and swore they would never take on themselves. When these feelings are stirred up in treatment, at times the patient behaves in subtly brutalizing ways to the therapist, who then may feel mistreated; at other times, the patient may dump these feelings inside the therapist. At these times, the therapist, rather than the patient, feels like and is pressured to behave like the mistreating caretaker, while the patient feels wronged."

Identifying the Totalistic Countertransference

"I think some of this might come clear," Harold went on, "if we focus on what's been transpiring between you and Nessie. We already know that part of your troublesome response reflects a classical countertransference reaction. Her pleas and suicidal concerns unconsciously reminded you of Phil, and you've reacted to her with those now-stirred-up dormant needs of rescuing and hating that really belonged to your relationship with him.

"Within the totalistic countertransference," Harold explained, "you've had two vacillating experiences that were just outside of your awareness. One set is that of experiencing *yourself* as being increasingly hopeless about aiding her and being helplessly intruded on by her, while simultaneously experiencing *her* as behaving in very controlling ways.

"This feeling of yours—of feeling pessimistic—can be therapeutically useful. You can use it as an empathic tool to communicate to Nessie your understanding of *her* hopelessness. I suggest that rather than reassuring her over and over again as you have been doing, you begin to put into words your understanding—born of your own experience—of how hopeless she feels. You might say something like 'This is a terrible time for you. You feel hopeless and believe that the person on whom you're depending—me—hasn't been able to relieve your very real suffering. And I think you see me as not really understanding how terrible you feel at times.'

"Putting into words her experience of the therapeutic relationship will allow her to feel more understood, and when she feels more understood, this will strengthen the working alliance between you. And this should allow her to feel more connected to you. This is particularly important, since for her connections and losses are so significant.

"I think that when you reassure her too much, you promote the opposite feeling: she feels you don't understand how terrible she is or you wouldn't be reassuring her."

Harold continued, "You can also use the other set of feelings in a similar way. In this set of feelings you experience yourself as angry toward her. I think as you become more aware of how angry you are toward Nessie for 'not getting better' and for interrupting your sleep, you'll be less pressured to act these feelings out through forgetting appointments. And you can use your understanding of these feelings of anger at being so intruded on and controlled, for example, by gently attempting to explore whether under her compliant waiflike style there hides much anger. I believe that Nessie's compliance defends against her anger at being dropped by Ralph, abandoned by her father, and intruded on by her mother. I think that she has difficulty tolerating, identifying, and expressing such anger lest those on whom she depends abandon her. And I think she 'put into you' this anger that she is unable to deal with."

"Oh," I broke in, "I'm beginning to understand. She puts into and stimulates anger within me, because she is unable to tolerate the idea of having these kinds of feelings. To her it's proof of her badness. And to her, expressing these feelings risks losing yet again another important figure. As I become aware of the anger she 'puts into me,' I can use this therapeutically by beginning cautiously to explore whether she keeps buried and hidden from herself unacceptable anger."

"Right."

"But what could I say to explore this?"

"Well, you might say something like 'You know, Nessie, at times I wonder whether you might be understandably irritated at me for not being able to help you as much as you want—but I have the feeling it would be hard for you to recognize, let alone express, even appropriate feelings of irritation.'"

"That's helpful," I admitted.

"Well, our time's just about up," Harold said, glancing at his watch. "But I want to make one important point before we stop. When a therapist is aware of having particularly difficult feelings toward a patient—such as being angry or being sexually attracted—he must attempt to differentiate what he's bringing to the table from what the patient may be putting into him. Therapists ought not to assume that they are having a totalistic countertransference reaction—that is, that the patient is 'putting' these feelings into them—when in fact they are having a 'classical' countertransference reaction—reflecting emerging feelings that are theirs and have remained dormant within them. Usually, therapists experience a blend of both classical and totalistic countertransference responses. And it's important for the therapist to understand what he's contributing to this blend and how much the patient is contributing."

NESSIE
(CONTINUED)

I found the consultation with Harold to be quite helpful. Understanding my own personal concerns around Uncle Phil allowed me to feel less pressure to "save" Nessie. As a result, I was able to put more appropriate—and clinically indicated—boundaries around our therapeutic relationship. After exploring these changes during our sessions, I was able to start seeing her once a week instead of three times and was able to limit appropriately her phoning me at home.

Making use of the information on totalistic countertransference, I was able to use some of my own feelings of helplessness and frustration to voice how helpless she felt about getting better and how at times she experienced me as not understanding the depths of her worries. Empathically commenting on her despair and fear that I did not understand did far more to comfort Nessie than any other reassurances I had previously felt pressured to offer.

Once I felt more aware of and comfortable with my feelings, I was also able to use my totalistic countertransference experiences to explore gingerly with Nessie her thinly veiled anger that she had previously kept herself unaware of, as well as her subtle but profound controlling behavior that had previously been cloaked by her compliance. As both of us understood more of the scenario that was playing out between us, Nessie gained more control over her behavior and distress.

And so did I.

LEARNING TO IDENTIFY
COUNTERTRANSFERENCE RESPONSES

I learned a lot from my consultation with Harold and from my treatment of Nessie. I learned that these feelings we term *countertransference* are common. The feelings themselves are not bad. What can be deleterious is when the therapist is unaware of these feelings and they prompt him to behave in antitherapeutic ways toward his clients.

So what is central to containing and learning from countertransference responses is our ability to spot these issues as they begin to emerge in therapy—before they cause damage.

From my ongoing discussions with Harold, I came to realize that there are two crucial elements that we therapists should focus on in order to spot our countertransference responses.

Introspective Curiosity

The first element that is absolutely essential in order for us to be aware of our countertransference is something called *introspective curiosity*. This is the capacity not only to listen to the patient but also to listen to ourselves, to the fantasies and behaviors that arise in the context of treating our clients.

In other words, I now continually monitor why I'm saying this or doing that. What I want to know is whether my comments and behavior are clinically indicated or whether they have more to do with my own needs, interests, curiosity, or comfort. Am I asking a particular client about the price he paid for a camera because I'm attempting to understand whether his judgment and impulsivity are improving? Or because I'm interested in cameras and I'd like to know where I might get the best deal? The former is in the best interests of the client, the latter an expression of my own countertransference rivalry.

This attitude of introspective curiosity is a general way of keeping tabs on my ongoing thoughts, feelings, and behavior toward my clients.

The Therapeutic Frame

In addition to this curiosity about my ongoing feelings and behavior to my clients, there are specific areas that I find particularly useful to monitor, and these are the areas that make up the therapeutic frame or structure of treatment.

What do I mean by frame or structure? Treating patients in psychotherapy requires certain structures or parameters that allow the patient to feel comfortable enough to talk about her innermost thoughts. These structures consist of the following principles: that the therapist and patient engage in speaking, rather than touching or holding; that the therapist addresses the patient consistently, not as "Nessie" on some occasions and "Ms. Smith" arbitrarily on other occasions; that the therapist's role is primarily to listen and talk about the patient's issues rather than about his own; that there is a defined, consistent, and predictable length to each session (the therapist meets the patient for, say, forty minutes each time and not five minutes sometimes and an hour at other times); that there is a defined, consistent, and predictable frequency of contact (the therapist doesn't arbitrarily meet once a week sometimes and once a month at other times); and that there is a defined and understood duration of treatment.

What I want to emphasize is that we therapists should be *particularly* curious about any arbitrary shift in this frame. If I find that I'm talking more about myself and my own issues than the patient's, this signals a countertransference response. If I'm seeing a particular patient three times a week, while I see every other patient once a week, this is a situation that I should also be curious about. Am I doing this because it's clinically indicated, or am I doing it for other reasons that are not that clear and may represent countertransference responses?

If I call all my patients by their first name but I find that I'm calling one patient Ms. Doe, I should be curious about why. Is it clinically indicated, or does it represent a countertransference response? For example, in this situation, I may be keeping myself unaware of how attracted I am to this patient and, without realizing why, attempting to distance myself through the formality of calling her Ms. Doe.

Overstepping other boundaries may also signal countertransference difficulties. A therapist who finds himself dreaming consistently about one particular patient but never about others should be aware of the existence of a countertransference issue. Similarly, a therapist who finds himself gossiping about certain patients should have similar concerns.

Another question I find useful is "Would I feel comfortable telling a colleague about my behavior with this patient?" If it's difficult for me to answer yes, I figure there are countertransference issues going on between that patient and me.

ONGOING CONTAINMENT OF COUNTERTRANSFERENCE

In discussing the issue of countertransference with some of my colleagues, I recognized that I was not alone in finding it difficult to identify these issues by myself. From these discussions, as well as from the consultation with Harold, I realized that there are three useful formats that can help identify, contain, and manage countertransference reactions before they jeopardize treatment.

Peer Supervision Groups

One of the most useful methods for understanding countertransference reactions is to form a peer supervision group. This group consists of anywhere from six to ten like-minded members who meet once a month in an ongoing way. The members discuss patients that they experience as troubling and difficult. Then they and the other group members attempt to understand what is happening.

In such a group it is important that members have similar levels of training, a psychodynamic orientation, and an ability to monitor their own levels of competitiveness and envy. The discussions should be conducted in an open, collegial, uncritical manner. And the members should make a commitment to meet for at least one year.

In groups where the members have little psychodynamic knowledge, it's often quite helpful to hire a psychoanalyst or analytically oriented clinician to offer some didactic information on psychodynamic concepts and to function as a facilitator for the group. This process of facilitation will ensure that the group maintains its collegial, open atmosphere, that issues of competitiveness are monitored, and that the focus remains on the therapist-patient interactions rather than on the personal lives of the therapists in the group.

Therapists in communities that do not have access to such a facilitator can often arrange for ongoing telephone conference-call supervision. Though at times this feels awkward and certainly has its limitations, it can be done and brings with it significant benefits.

Professional Meetings

Specific meetings of local, regional, and national discipline-based organizations (such as the annual meetings of the American Psychological Association, the American Psychiatric Association, and so on) often have sections that focus on psychotherapy. Usually issues related to countertransference are presented.

Personal Therapy

Recently one of my colleagues said to me, "I found the peer supervision group that we formed to be very useful. It has opened my eyes to a lot of blind spots I have with clients. But I've become aware that I have an ongoing problem with older male clients. I get passive, start daydreaming, and tune out. It's funny that I've just become aware of this, because in retrospect, it seems I've always done it. The group has certainly opened my eyes to that. However, I can't seem to get around it, and I decided about six months ago to go into treatment myself. It's been really helpful. It has allowed me to get over that withdrawal from certain clients. I've also noticed that I've been able to stand up for myself a lot better with the director of the clinic."

In some situations, when difficulties around a particular type of patient occur repetitively, individual therapy is also a helpful option.

∽

I've come to realize that countertransference responses to the difficult personality-disordered patient are quite common. I've also come to realize that such feelings in themselves aren't "bad." The only harm they cause is when they remain unknown, as mine were about Nessie. In this situation they can invisibly but profoundly derail treatment. My seeing Nessie too frequently, allowing her to call me at home, and being unable to set appropriate limits are examples.

It was only when I was able to tease apart those issues that I brought to the table—such as my need to rescue her as an expression of my dormant but still alive feelings around my uncle Phil—that I was able to behave more therapeutically. My treatment of her also benefited from my understanding what she brought to the table—those feelings and relationships she "dumped" into me so that both of us would replay a traumatic relationship that had occurred earlier between her and her caretakers. It was through understanding this older relationship via my countertransference that I was able to talk to her about her veiled anger and her hidden controlling behaviors. This understanding also allowed me to make more empathic statements to her so that she felt more understood, rather than falsely reassured.

I know now, too, the importance of listening to myself as well as listening to my patients and of attempting to understand my responses as a reflection of my past, as well as of the past that the patient puts into me, so that ultimately I can use this knowledge to further my patient's healing.

NOTES

P. 180, *a book I had read recently:* Hawkins, P., & Shohet, R. (1994). *Supervision in the helping professions.* Philadelphia: Open University Press.

P. 181, *"Countertransference refers to dormant feelings":* Greenson, R. R. (1967). *The technique and practice of psychoanalysis.* New York: International Universities Press.

P. 181, *the 'totalistic' countertransference:* Kernberg, O. (1975). *Borderline conditions and pathological narcissism.* New York: Jason Aronson.

P. 186, *Glen Gabbard:* Gabbard, G., & Wilkinson, S. M. (1994). *Management of countertransference with borderline patients.* Washington, DC: American Psychiatric Press.

P. 189, *Only when the therapist has 'passed':* Weiss, J. (1990). Unconscious mental functioning. *Scientific American, 263,* 103–109.

P. 198, *something called* introspective curiosity: Book, H. E. (1987). The resident's countertransference: Approaching an avoided topic. *American Journal of Psychotherapy, 41,* 555–562.

P. 199, *What do I mean by frame or structure?:* Epstein, R. S. (1994). *Keeping boundaries.* Washington, DC: American Psychiatric Press.

ABOUT THE AUTHORS

Alan Bardikoff, Ph.D., is a psychologist in private practice and on the staff of the Day Treatment Program at Toronto East General Hospital. An adjunct supervisor in the Department of Applied Psychology, Ontario Institute of Studies in Education, University of Toronto, he also consults to several children's mental health agencies in Toronto.

Howard E. Book, M.D., D.Psych., FRCPC, FAPA, is a clinician, lecturer, author, and consultant in the field of psychodynamic psychotherapy. He is currently director of the Brief Psychotherapy Training Program, University of Toronto/Women's College Hospital; a senior psychotherapy consultant, Inpatient Services, Toronto Hospital; and a consultant to the Clarke Institute of Psychiatry. Dr. Book holds an associate professorship in the Department of Psychiatry and the Department of Health Administration in the Faculty of Medicine at the University of Toronto.

Timothy Davis, M.D., is an assistant psychiatrist at McLean Hospital and an instructor in psychiatry at Harvard Medical School. He is actively involved in the Ambulatory Borderline Services and is psychiatrist-in-charge of the Women's Treatment Program, a partial hospital program specializing in the care of women with posttraumatic, dissociative, and severe personality disorders.

Allen Frances, M.D., is chair of the Department of Psychiatry and Behavioral Sciences at Duke University. He was chair of the *DSM-IV* Task Force and is the editor of the *Journal of Practical Psychiatry and Behavioral Health*.

John G. Gunderson, M.D., conducted the seminal work that defined Borderline Personality Disorder and that prompted enormous growth in its clinical recognition and research. He is director of psychosocial research and the Ambulatory Borderline Services at McLean Hospital. He is a professor in psychiatry at Harvard Medical School.

Caroline Haynes, M.D., Ph.D., is director of medical student education in psychiatry at Duke University Medical Center and is the coordinator of the Post-Graduate Year One (PGY-I) residency curriculum. Her areas of interest include the diagnosis and treatment of mood disorders, the interaction of personality factors with mood disorders, and supportive approaches to the management of personality disorders in psychiatric and nonpsychiatric settings.

Sam Izenberg, M.D., is an adult and child psychiatrist and psychoanalyst with a special interest in the teaching of psychotherapy. He is director of psychotherapy training at The Toronto Hospital and vice president at the Institute for the Advancement of Self Psychology.

Jerome Kroll, M.D., is professor of psychiatry at the University of Minnesota Medical School and vice president of the Association for the Advancement of Philosophy and Psychiatry. He has written *The Challenge of the Borderline Patient* (1988) and *PTSD/Borderlines in Therapy: Finding the Balance* (1993) and has co-authored *The Reality of Mental Illness* (with Sir Martin Roth, 1986).

Gary Rodin, M.D., is psychiatrist-in-chief at The Toronto Hospital and professor of psychiatry at the University of Toronto. He is also a psychoanalyst with long-standing interests in psychotherapy and in disorders of subjective experience. Dr. Rodin has conducted research and published in the areas of psychotherapy, self psychology, and psychosomatic medicine.

Michael Rosenbluth, M.D., is psychiatrist-in-chief of the Department of Psychiatry at Toronto East General Hospital, psychotherapy consultant at Sunnybrook Health Science Center, and assistant professor at the University of Toronto Medical School. He is co-editor of *The Handbook of Borderline Disorders* (with Daniel Silver, 1992).

Robert G. Ruegg, M.D., is head of the Personality Disorders and Substance Abuse Section of the Adult Admissions Unit of John Umstead State Psychiatric Hospital in Butner, North Carolina, and is assistant consulting professor in biological psychiatry at Duke University Medical Center in Durham, North Carolina. He has lectured and published scientific articles about the psychobiology of depression and personality disorders, substance abuse, the dually diagnosed, and the education of psychiatric residents.

Daniel Silver, M.D., is clinical consultant to the Department of Psychiatry, Mount Sinai Hospital, and associate professor at the University of Toronto Medical School. He is a member of the Canadian Institute of Psychoanalysis and co-editor of *The Handbook of Borderline Disorders* (with Michael Rosenbluth, 1992).

Virginia R. Youngren, Ph.D., is a member of the staff of the Ambulatory Borderline Services and Adult Outpatient Clinic at McLean Hospital, where she specializes in long-term therapy with adults who have trauma histories and personality disorders.

INDEX